Albania: the Cost

Albania: the Cost

Albanian Evangelical Mission
Wrexham

Quinta Press
Weston Rhyn
MMVII

Quinta Press

Meadow View, Weston Rhyn, Oswestry, Shropshire, England, SY10 7RN

Visit our web-site: http://www.quintapress.com

ISBN 978 1 897856 28 4

Published on behalf of Albanian Evangelical Mission,
29 Bridge Street, Penybryn, Wrexham, LL13 7HP

Web-site www.aemission.org

Cover drawing by Ian Steadman

Preface

The cost of bringing the Gospel to the Albanian people has always been high. This book looks at some of the people who have made the attempt, both Albanian and foreign, and the price they have had to pay.

The title (and the cover drawing) are based on the Lord's parable of the man who began to build a tower without first sitting down "to count the cost, whether he has enough to complete it". He laid the foundation, but was not able to finish, and his work was left incomplete and his good name demeaned.

This book is offered in the hope that its readers will be stirred to follow the example of those who did pay the full price required of them. When God calls us, we must count the cost and be willing to see the work through to the end: it may require our all, but we cannot honourably offer less for Him who gave all for us, and calls us to follow His example and the example of some who have gone before, in obedience to His calling and command.

Contents

The chapters are arranged chronologically. The names are those of the main contributor to each chapter.

Note: The extracts from the publications of the British and Foreign Bible Society have been left unchanged, except that in them I have standardised the spelling of *han* and *hanjee.* In Turkish these are spelled han and hancı, in Albanian han and hanxhi. In older English publications they are given a variety of renderings; I have chosen these two, simply because they are my personal preference. In a similar way, the word for a Moslem cleric (hoca in Turkish, hoxha in Albanian) I have anglicised to hoja.—David Young

---

* Parts of these sections appeared in our previous book *Battle for Albania* (and, in Albanian, *Ungjilli ndër Shqiptarët*). Extracts from Alexander Thomson's unpublished Agent's Books (numbers 117, 127 and 133) are quoted with permission from the Bible Society Library, at the Cambridge University Library, for which we express our gratitude.

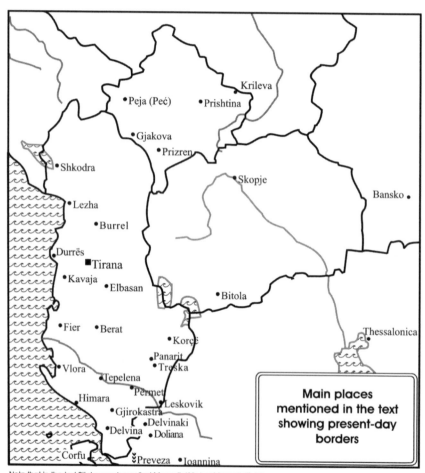

Note that in the text Bitola may be called Monastir (Alb.) or Manastir (Turk.)

Map drawn by David J. Neal, Wrexham

Prelude: the sub-apostolic period

Christianity in Albania claims apostolic foundation, and Albania's geographical position makes this almost inevitable. The Christian gospel was first planted in Europe by the apostle Paul at Philippi in Macedonia. Travelling westward on the Via Egnatia he preached at Thessalonica, the largest city on this great highway. This became the centre from which Christianity radiated to Athens and Corinth, and to the province of Illyricum.

It is interesting to note how closely Paul's missionary journeys followed the Roman highways, and along them extends the chain of early churches. Indeed, a trip of 150 miles along the Egnatian highway from Thessalonica westward penetrates to the heart of Albania.

The apostle Paul travelled that road. On his third itinerary, about 59 AD, he wrote to the church at Rome that: "From Jerusalem, and round about unto Illyricum, I have fully preached the gospel of Christ". The Greek preposition "unto" is ambiguous, admitting either an exclusive or inclusive usage: it does not state certainly whether Paul had taken the gospel as far as the Illyrian frontier, or whether he had penetrated the province. But ancient tradition holds that Paul introduced Christianity into Albania.

Farlati, the Catholic historian, claimed that the church of Durrës was the most ancient in Albania, having been founded by the apostle Paul while preaching in Illyria and Epirus. He wrote that in 58 AD there were seventy Christian families at Durrës having for bishop one Caesar or Apollonius.

The Albanian Catholic Bulletin points out that the late Albanian scholar Faik Konica says in *Albania: the Rock Garden of Southeastern Europe* (Boston, 1960) that "As early as the year 58, the existence of an important Christian community at Durrës is on record."

There was also the visit of Titus. While imprisoned at Rome, Paul wrote that Titus had gone to Dalmatia (2 Tim. 4.10)—a name synonymous with Illyricum, and derived from the name of an Illyrian tribe which lived there.

During the post-apostolic period, information on the existence of Christian churches in Albania is unfortunately vague. Yet there were some Illyrian martyrs. Hyacinthe Hecquard (*Histoire et description de la Haute Albanie ou Guégarie*, Paris 1857) wrote that among the three bishops of the early church cited in Farlati's *Illyricum Sacrum*, the second, St Astius of Durrës, was martyred under the Emperor Trajan (A.D. 56-117),[1] together with seven Romans who had fled from persecution in Rome and sought refuge at Durrës.

According to the Albanian Catholic Bulletin (Vol. V, No. 1 & 2, 1984):

> Roman persecution of Christians in Illyria began early. The first Illyrian Christian martyrs, Florin and Laurin of Ulpiana (near Prishtinë, Yugoslavia), were put to death during the reign of Roman Emperor Hadrian (76-138 A.D.).[2] The persecution of the Christian Church of Illyria was continued by the Roman Emperor Diocletian (245-313 A.D.).[3]

It is strange that Illyrians were responsible both for the systematic persecution of Christianity, and later for its establishment as the official religion of the empire. The Illyrian emperor Decius undertook the first universal and most vicious persecution to stamp out Christianity. The great Diocletian made his native Salona, just above Shkodra, the administrative seat of the province Illyricum. He erected here his magnificent palace, and under imperial patronage the city rapidly flourished. Christianity in Illyricum seems also to have centered on Salona, where a wealth of inscriptions reveal a considerable Christian presence. Diocletian's reign was stained by bitter persecutions (303-311), instigated by two fanatical Illyrian colleagues, Maximian and Galerius, in which so many Christians died here that the authorities erected a monument bearing the Latin words "extincto nomine Christianorum" (The name of Christian is extinguished).

A year after the retirement of Diocletian in 305, another Illyrian, Constantine, became a Caesar then an Augustus. In 313 he issued his famous Edict of Milan guaranteeing religious toleration.

Thus, the first and last great persecutions of the Church, and the Church's peace, came alike from Illyrian hands.

---

1 He reigned 98-117 AD. 2 He reigned 117-138 AD. 3 He reigned 284-305 AD.

Bible Society Workers

In the second decade of the 19th century, after long years of darkness and neglect, God began to turn the minds of His people once more towards the needs of Albania. If you have read our previous book *Battle for Albania* (or its Albanian version, *Ungjilli ndër Shqiptarët*) you will be familiar with parts of this story.

In 1817, the British and Foreign Bible Society printed a letter written on 28th August, 1816, from the Rev. R. Pinkerton, in which he wrote:

"The furnishing of the Albanians with a New Testament at least, in their own language, is an object highly worthy of the attention of the British and Foreign Bible Society. They still have no part of the word of God in their own tongue. Or, should a Bible Society be established in one of the Ionian Islands, the giving to the Albanians a New Testament in their own tongue, would certainly become an object worthy of its earliest and most zealous efforts."

On 25th October 1819 he wrote to the Society again:

"a translation of the New Testament into the Albanian language has entwined itself about my heart for these several years past, in such a way that I literally could not get rid of it ..."

In 1822 the New Testament was being revised, but in 1824 it was reported that "Death has removed the original translator and the two priests who had been selected for the purpose of revising the version ..."

Others properly qualified for the task were found and by 1825 the revision was complete, and Matthew's Gospel was printed and put into circulation. Rev. Isaac Lowndes, Secretary of the Ionian Bible Society, reported that "a priest of this nation had called upon him to request a copy, saying, that he had received accounts from his country that many there were anxious to have the work."

Printing of the New Testament began in January, 1825, at Corfu.

In 1826 it was reported that the Gospel of Matthew had been "distributed and received with the greatest joy", and in 1828 that the complete New Testament, in parallel columns in Albanian and Modern Greek, had been finished under the supervision of the Rev.

Isaac Lowndes, at Corfu. From 1830 we read of distribution of the New Testament inside Albania.

In 1860, a highly providential event took place in the development of the work, when the British and Foreign Bible Society appointed a new agent at Constantinople to direct its operations in Turkey. The man chosen was the Rev. Alexander Thomson (1820-1899).

According to the Free Church of Scotland list of Ordained Ministers and Missionaries, Alexander Thomson was born at Edinburgh in 1820. Nothing is known of his childhood and youth, save that his father died when he was 6 years old.

He studied at the University of St Andrews and at New College, Edinburgh, and in 1845 was ordained as a missionary to the Jews. For two years he was stationed at Budapest, and then at Constantinople. He served as a missionary to the Jews for about sixteen years.

Then, a proposed change on the part of the Free Church with regard to the Jewish Mission at Constantinople led to his transfer to the Bible Society, to direct their operations in Turkey, which at that time included the province of Albania.

In 1863 he made a tour of Bosnia and Albania to ascertain for himself its spiritual condition and to judge the probable results of further efforts for the circulation of the scriptures in Albania. He reported that *"In all these extensive districts … there is no missionary whatever …"* The tour led the Society to the conviction that Thomson had been the means, under God, of opening a wide and effectual door for the entrance of the truth into a land shrouded in spiritual darkness.

There are instances of suffering and sacrifice which people made in the course of the work he led, not least among them:

Colporteur Fischer in Berat was heavily afflicted in the 1870s when his wife and daughter were stricken with fever—his daughter twice, so as to be brought almost to the grave—and was eventually compelled to leave the town.

Agent's Book 1873: "Poor Klundt has been sorely tried, since he went to Uscup [Skopje], the station for West Old Servia [Kosova] and North Macedonia. He first lost his eldest boy, then almost the whole family fell sick, himself severely affected with fever and the others with small pox of a bad type, of which a second child died.

They are better now, but he himself is still feeble. He is a truly Christian and zealous man."

In 1883, reports came from all parts of Alexander Thomson's agency (which included Albania) of maltreatment, persecution and even imprisonment endured by the Society's colporteurs. Colporteur Sevastides was arrested and expelled from Shkodër and made to walk on foot over flooded country behind a mounted policeman, lodging at various prisons on the way, till after thirteen days he returned home to Berat, where he was released. He was utterly exhausted, and confined to bed for some weeks. In August 1884, he was obliged to leave Albania owing to the dangerous illness of his wife.

Gjerasim Qiriazi, who planted the first Evangelical church in Albania,. was captured by outlaws and held as their prisoner. The Society reported that "much prayer was offered, and many exertions were made for his release. After five months of cruel treatment, his ransom was effected, and his return home, on April 30th, changed a meeting called for prayer on his behalf into one of praise." He died in 1894 aged 35, perhaps poisoned for his Gospel work (though this has not been established), perhaps owing to a ruined constitution from his months of captivity at the hands of the outlaws on a journey to Korçë ten years earlier, the story of which is told in his book *Captured by Brigands*.

Colporteur Michael, who had already been imprisoned several times, was struck a severe blow in Doliana, north of Janinë, which knocked him bleeding and unconscious to the ground, while his books were seized; this was the result of an episcopal circular against Protestants.

Elias Zarifzappas served as a Bible Society colporteur in Albania from 1910; in 1916 he was imprisoned and later condemned to forced labour; he resumed his work as a colporteur, and in 1920 he was discovered penniless and weak from lack of food; in 1926, when he was due for retirement, he disappeared in the interior of Albania and was never heard of again.

Alexander Thomson wrote in 1889 of the Society's "desire to penetrate into the uplands of Albania and Macedonia, the haunts of savage, bloodthirsty brigands who keep the land in terror."

Maybe one day the fuller story of the heroism, devotion and sufferings of the men and women who met these dangers and endured these sufferings will be told, but we shall concentrate on just three of the Bible Society's men who paid a high price to bring the knowledge of Christ to that land and people.

Alexander Davidson

Alexander Davidson, a young man from Edinburgh, was stationed at Janinë—then the capital of southern Albania—in May 1865, where he stayed until 1870 before being transferred to Crete.

In May he reported a stir among the Jewish population of Janinë, to whom a monument is to be seen opposite the walls of the old city. One of their number had become a Christian, a young man of one of the chief families. His friends attempted to strangle him, and spread a report that he was insane. Davidson was told that he was in the cathedral one Sunday morning, busy making the sign of the Cross "and other outward demonstrations". On a Friday evening, forty Jews met at his father's house, collected his clothes, put them in a heap in the court, placed on them a paper with his name and age written on it, and set fire to the lot. They then each ate half an egg and threw the other half on to the burning pile, whilst heaping curses upon him and wishing that he would die within forty days. As this happened so close in time to Davidson's arrival in the city, it led to the circulation of strange fancies, as that he had come to make Protestants of both Orthodox and Moslems, "doubtless by some mysterious process".

Nonetheless, at first his depot was crowded with visitors from morning till evening, eager to read or buy the scriptures, and he sold about two hundred copies there. He wrote, "Most of the sales have been to Greeks and Jews ... As yet, very few of the Albanian scriptures have been sold, as scarcely any of the native Albanians can read." At this stage, he met with no incivility or disrespect.

As visits to the depot reduced, he decided it was time to begin colportage in surrounding areas. Interest varied from place to place, but he wrote that "I have seen many of them sitting in their shops reading the Word." He planned to travel more widely from September onwards: "With God's blessing, we hope to visit every considerable town and village of Epirus with the Word of God, and thus sowing the good seed, we doubt not that, 'in due time, we shall reap, if we fail not.'"

In August 1866 the following report from him was published in the Bible Society's *Monthly Reporter*. It is important to bear in mind that when he writes "Christian" he is usually referring to the Greek Orthodox community rather than to people's inward personal convictions. In addition, there used to be a practice of dubbing all Greek Orthodox Albanians as "Greeks", and we cannot tell whether Davidson sometimes uses the word "Greeks" to denote Albanians belonging to that religious body. The report reads:

Twelve months since a Depot was established, with the sanction of the Committee, at Ioannina, the capital of Southern Albania. The Rev. Dr. Thomson, of Constantinople, had been desirous for some time to have a sub-Agency at this important centre, and having secured the services of Mr. A. G. Davidson, the necessary arrangements were completed. As the work to be done in Ioannina itself could not occupy the whole of Mr. Davidson's time, it was determined, that whenever practicable he should undertake colportage tours in the surrounding country, visiting the towns and villages, where few efforts have been previously made, to induce the people, who are very mixed as regards their religious beliefs, to purchase the Scriptures. The following letter records the difficulties and experiences of Mr. Davidson during a recent journey. It will be seen that much apathy and bigotry had to be encountered. Great results, numerically, were not to be anticipated in this commencement of the work; but it is hoped that the good seed has been cast upon some soil in which it will germinate and bear fruit to the glory of God:—

I set out from Ioannina on the morning of the 22nd March, having to hire means of conveyance to Argyro Castro [Gjirokastër], as no horses were to be had at Delvinaki, bargaining with the muleteer to remain a day at the last-mentioned place. After a ride of ten hours, a shower of rain compelled us to take shelter at four P.M. in the village of Móshori. It is a small village, about a quarter of an hour from the road. I soon had most of the men of the place in the han, anxious to know what I had. Those of them who could read did so for the benefit of others, as well as for themselves. I could, however, effect no sales among them. There is a school of twenty or twenty-five boys in Móshori. Next morning we left early for Delvinaki, distant about four hours. On the way we had a heavy shower of rain for fully two hours. Delvinaki has two schools, one of about eighty children, taught by two teachers; the other, eighteen scholars, taught, by one teacher, who purchased an ancient Greek New Testament. Several men of the place came and read the Scriptures where I was, and three or four wanted to purchase, but would not give the price I asked. No men were to be seen working—all walking idly about, with a stick in their hand, while the women were busy driving stones, &c, with horses. There being no han, and none of the people seeming to take any more interest in what I was offering to their notice, I set off to Xeróvalto, three hours distant, to spend the night. I sold an Albanian Gospel to the boy at the han. The village is away on the opposite side up the mountain slope, near to which is another village, called Pondikáti. There is a Turkish village, having a mudiri,[1] round the corner of the mountain. I was detained for some time here next morning by the hanjee, who seized the horse because I would not give him ten piastres for my night's lodgings. I appealed to a policeman who was staying there, but he took the part of the hanjee. I offered three and a half piastres to get away, which he would not take until I said I would go on foot, and report them both to the Caimakan at Argyro Castro, which made them willing to take what I had offered. I remained a short time at Episkopi, but none of the people wanted any of my books. Here I had a view of the villages lying along the side of the fertile plain of Derópuli [Dropulli], south of Argyro Castro, twelve of which I afterwards visited. I got to Argyro Castro about three P.M. on Saturday. Having a letter from the Pasha of Ioannina, which Major Stuart kindly got for me, as well as a buyurdi,[2] I went up to the Caimakan on Monday morning. Having presented the letter to him, he asked what I was going to do there. I told him, and showed him one of the handsomely-bound Turkish New Testaments, which I had in my pocket, which he purchased, and asked me to bring up some of the

---

1 Turkish müdìr, official governing a subdistrict.
2 Albanian bujurdi (from Turkish): an official order.

other books to show to him. I took up a few, but when I returned the Bishop was with him, and I could not see him afterwards. His clerk bought a Greek Bible, and an ancient Greek New Testament. Several persons about the castle wanted a copy like that purchased by the Caimakan, but unfortunately I had not taken another with me. One gentleman bought a Turkish Genesis and Psalms; a Turkish Testament, 16mo., ten piastres; and a French Bible; another, a Turkish Testament, six piastres; another, a Turkish Gospel and Acts, 16mo., four piastres; and a policeman an Albanian Matthew. Thus the way being led by the Caimakan's example, I sold nine copies at the castle that day. I sent to Ioannina for a few copies of those Scriptures which they wanted; but when I received them I could not find the persons who had formerly asked for them. Great numbers of Moslems came to me in the han, Beys and Hojas among the rest, but I could get none of them to purchase. They put some strange questions to me. One of them gave as a reason why Mohammed is greater than Christ, that the Arabic language contains more letters than the Hebrew. They don't believe in the omnipresence of God. On the Sabbath after my arrival, I had a visit from a Turkish medical student from Constantinople, belonging to this place, who appears anxious to become a Protestant. He mentioned the name of one Mr. Charles, of Constantinople. I could not gather from him any sufficient reason why he wished to renounce the faith of the Prophet. It seems he still frequents the mosques.

The Christian part of the population stood aloof from me. During my stay I could not get one New Testament sold among them. On glancing at the first page, and not seeing the seal of the Patriarch, they would not look within. On the day of my arrival, one of them asked me if I was one of the propaganda from Ioannina, telling me there were seven of us in Ioannina, for the purpose of winning over the Greek Christians to Protestantism. The report is current among them, that the British Government gives to each Turk who becomes Protestant 8*l.*, and an annual sum afterwards. The hanjee said he saw them receive it when he was at Constantinople. I did not like to denounce him as a liar to his face, but I told him I did not believe he was speaking the truth. With the utmost watchfulness I had two books stolen from me one day, an Arabic Gospel and Acts, and an Albanian Epistles. I saw an Italian doctor, whose acquaintance Dr.

Thomson had made when in Argyro Castro. He had been confined to bed for six weeks. He showed me a copy of the Albanian Epistles, with Dr. Thomson's name written on the fly leaf; but I am sorry to say neither it nor the Italian Bible had the appearance of being much used. During the first week of my stay the weather was rather rainy, and on the following Tuesday, the weather being good, I hired a horse to visit the villages of Derópoli. These villages all lie close to each other, the furthest off I visited, Serváti, being six hours from Argyro Castro. On the 3rd I got to Sofratiká, three hours distant. I made my way to the church, where I found the priest acting as teacher to twenty-two children, at the same time busy mending his stockings. He purchased a Greek Diglot Testament, 12mo., and would have purchased a Greek Bible, had I given it for fifteen piastres. The priest from the next village was also there, who purchased a Greek Testament, 12mo. They will not give the English, and Protestants in general, the honour of the Christian name, calling them idolatrous heathen.

I next came to Tereeacháti [Terihat], and learning there was to be a funeral soon, I took up my position, in the churchyard. The two priests whom I had seen at the other village were officiating at the funeral, assisted by another priest. The people stood aloof at first; but I had the privilege of selling two Albanian St Matthew, one Albanian Epistles, one Modern Greek Testament, 32mo. After the interment, bread, boiled wheat and wine were handed round to the people. The village has a good schoolhouse, but no teacher at present.

The next village was Góritza [Gorica]. There were no men in it, all being busy down in the plain. It possesses neither priest or school.

The next village was Vrástani [Frashtani]. I entered a shop within the churchyard, and the priest was soon sent for. I found him the most bigoted person in all these villages. Yet he purchased an Albanian St Matthew; but I could get none of the others to purchase. There is no school here.

The next village was Léwgari [Lugar]. Here, as in the two last villages, the men were all away in the fields. I found the priest, an old man, but he would not purchase unless I would give him a ten-piastre Testament for three piastres.

We spent the night at Gárbushi [Grapshi], on the road from Delvino to Ioannina. It is a scattered village on both sides of the gorge. The han is far from being enticing. Early next morning I canvassed the village along with the muleteer, a Turk, who was very intent on recommending the Scriptures to the people. I found the priest, the schoolmaster, and a few more at the church; but could not effect any sales. After the first day I sold none among these villages. From fifteen to twenty boys attend the school.

The next village was Yurgudsáti [Jergucat], a considerable village up a gorge. There are four or five children taught by the priest.

We next came to Serváti [Zervati], where I prepared a cup of coffee under a tree. I found the priest here rather more charitably disposed than the others. He pleaded want of money to purchase, as did also the others. I then retraced my steps to Argyro Castro, stopping at Douvianí [Dhuvjani], a large village, possessing good houses. There is a large school here, having about fifty scholars. The teacher had got a Bible from the Depot at Athens, as had also two men, who kindly took me to their house and gave me a cup of coffee. The houses are of a better construction than in any of the other villages.

I then made for Goranzí [Goranxia], where I stayed for the night. It and the next are the two largest villages on this side of the plain. I had a goodly number looking at the Scriptures, but not coming through the 'Great Church' was quite sufficient for them. The schoolhouse is a new building, but the teacher was away to keep his Easter holidays.

The next village was Dervitsháni [Derviçani]. Here one man, calling himself a doctor, took away a New Testament; but instead of bringing back the price of it, he brought back the book, saying it was full of errors. The only one he could point out was in the temptation of Jesus, where it says 'he was an hungered.' I asked him to compare it with the Testament in the church close by, and he would find the same error there, if error it was. He backed out by saying it had not the sanction of the Patriarch.

I next went up the hill to Lezerátes [Lazarati], a Turkish village, one hour from Argyro Castro. None of those whom I saw could read a single letter.

The following day, Friday, I crossed the plain to Libóchovo, the largest of all these villages. It contains very few Christians, the one side of the plain being of Christian population, the other

Mahommedan. It was market-day, so I went to the market-place, and was soon surrounded. The muleteer kept a strict watch over the books, lest any of them should be stolen. I only managed to sell one copy, an Albanian Matthew.

I had a ride of seven hours to Tepeleni on Tuesday, and fifteen hours yesterday to this place (Avlona [Vlora]). The Christians would not purchase from me in Tepeleni, not having the sanction of the Patriarch. As to what success I may have here, I cannot say, having got in last night, and it is not yet midday. The mails leave at two to-day, so I had to write early. At present I purpose to stay here until Monday, and then, if I can get horses, to go down the seaboard among the villages, six of which I hope to be able to visit. I shall probably have to hire from this for three days, there being no horses to be got in those villages, nor is there any han.

I am not certain but that I may go from Delvino [Delvinë] to Philates, &c., down to Prevesa, returning by the valley of the Luro.

In Avlona I found the people far more opposed to purchasing the Scriptures than I had expected. Very few came to my quarters in the han; but when I went out through the bazaar I was soon surrounded. It was some time ere I could get a single copy sold as a commencement; but at last a gentleman purchased an Italian Testament, and, having once made a beginning, another purchased an Albanian Gospel, another a Greek Bible; but then an influential person started up, declaring that the books they were about to purchase were erroneous, whereas, when I called upon him to point out where the errors were, he would not do so, but removed to a short distance. In consequence of that, I could not do anything more among them. In the han I sold a Turkish New Testament to a travelling Turkish doctor, whose acquaintance I made in Argyro Castro. I went up to the serai[3] with a few copies; offered them for sale there; but the Pasha not purchasing, none of the others would. I stayed in Avlona until Monday morning. A leading man among the Greek community was highly displeased with the Albanian Epistles, for, on turning to the Epistle to the Romans, he found it there stated that Christ is of the seed of David, which he denies, many affirming here, as well as in other places, that Jesus was a Greek.

---

3 Turkish sarày, government house.

It was raining when we left Avlona, and we reached Dukátes [Dukati] after a nine hours' ride, and as there was no regular han, we were received into a small shop, where five of us rested all night, in a space of about eight feet square. The village is much scattered; has no school; is entirely Turkish, with the exception of two Greek merchants, to one of whom I sold a Modern Greek New Testament.

I left Dukátes at ten A.M., and after riding for fully two hours up the ravine, among Scotch and spruce fir-trees, arrived at the pass of Tschika [Çika]. About half-way up is a small saw-mill, worked by water power, and as we were passing we heard the trees come crashing down the side of the mountain, in obedience to the woodman's axe. From the pass a most magnificent view is to be had. Looking behind is the bay of Avlona, with its island in the distance, seen through the gap up which we came to Dukates; on the other hand, the snow-clad Tschika; and in front, Corfu and its small islands; while further away in the distance a dim glimpse of Italy is to be had. The path, after crossing the summit, runs along the side of the mountain a great height up; while looking down the side of the mountain the sea is lying at its base. I got to Paliása [Palasa] about three in the afternoon. It is a small village, and has no school. The population here, and as far as Chimara, are all Christian. There is no han, but I got into the house of the resident merchant. I very soon had the men of the place around me, very few of whom could read. Not being able to effect any sales, I departed early next morning, having had difficulty in procuring mules.

The road to Drymades [Dhërmiu] is very bad. According to my bargain I stopped an hour there. It is the largest of these Chimariot villages, possessing a good school. I should have gone to it from Dukates had I received true information. I should have sold a few copies there, but never having had anything to do with fixed prices, the people would not give the price, although they confessed the books were exceedingly cheap. In about two hours after we got to Vunó, a large wealthy village, superior in education to the other villages, but I could not get the people so much as to look at the Scriptures, much less to purchase. Finding it of no avail to stay there, I set off for Chimara, which we reached a little after mid-day, and I got into the merchant's house to stay, and was treated very kindly. Two young men purchased each an Albanian Epistle; one of them, however, trying to pass a bad coin upon me. There is a school, but, at the time of my visit, there was no schoolmaster. Not being able to find any horses to go to the intermediate villages, I had to proceed straight to Delvino, a ride of twelve hours. The chief villages on the way are Peekérasi [Peqeras], Aghia, Vasili and Nivítza. I got to Delvino on Thursday, and remained there till Monday. Saturday being the weekly market-day, I went out like others, and placed my books on the stones among butter, cheese, flour, &c. The people were not long in coming to see what the Franco had for sale, but, as everywhere else, the report spread that they were false books. However, I was privileged to sell two Turkish New Testaments, and in the evening a few of the Greeks came to the han, to whom I sold three copies of the Albanian Epistles. Several came on the Sabbath to see the books, which I do not expose on that day, so, after a little conversation, they left me.

I departed from Delvino at half-past nine A.M. on Monday, reaching the small Turkish village of Makati [Markat?] that night; slept in a small Greek shop, and next day reached Philates at noon, a distance of about sixteen hours from Delvino. On the way, about four hours from Philates, are two considerable villages, the largest called Pleeshóvitza. On my arrival, the people seemed to stand aloof from me; but towards night, as I was on my way to get something for my evening meal, I saw an Aigumenos[4] from the Monastery of St George, about an hour from Ioannina. After saluting each other, he came with me to the han, followed by a crowd, to see what his verdict upon the Scriptures would be; but he not only assured the people that they were quite correct, but purchased a Greek New Testament, calling upon them to do likewise. Next day he came in the morning to see me, and although he appeared somewhat shocked at my not praying to, or believing in, the intercession of the Virgin, he afterwards brought two Greek merchants and prevailed upon them to purchase a Greek Bible and an Ancient New Testament each; so that, chiefly through his influence, I was enabled to sell twenty copies there. He also removed the obstacle to the fixed price, by assuring them that such was my custom in Ioannina. He was on his round visiting the churches and monasteries as far as Delvino.

---

4 Greek ηγούμενος abbot, prior.

I left for Paramythia on Friday, so as to be in time for the Saturday market. We had to cross a rather deep river on our way, the water coming up to the horse's girths; but the rest of the road is tolerably good.

On Saturday I took up my stand in the market-place, in a commanding position, but few of the Greeks would come near me. Large numbers of Mahommedans came and read, but made no purchases. To the son of the hanjee I sold a New Testament, and the Prophets, two Psalms and the Pentateuch to a Jew, having had better success than last autumn; while in Margariti I fared the same as then, the people having made up their minds not to purchase, let me come as often as I may. In Parga I sold two Hebrew Psalms and one 12mo. Bible, but the Greeks would not become customers. One Turkish soldier tried to get a bad coin palmed upon me for a Turkish Gospel and Acts. This time I went to the han, and found it more convenient and comfortable than the room I occupied during my former visit.

On Thursday, May 3rd, I embarked in a small boat for Prevesa, reaching it in seven hours, whereas last time it took us two days between the two places. Here I found the people as much in opposition as during my former visit, and could not do anything among them until Monday forenoon, when I sold three Ancient Greek New Testaments to the clerk at the Greek Consulate. I left for Ioannina on Monday evening at four; rode five hours; slept in the open air; then started about half-past two next morning, passed the village of Luro, composed of about thirty or forty houses constructed of wicker-work, and there are a few other villages along the road of fifteen and twenty houses, but none of any size. We rode till eleven A.M., rested till four, rode six hours, and got to Ioannina next day at ten A.M., having travelled six hours. Thus my tour has lasted seven weeks, during which I have disposed of sixty-five copies, and Mrs. Davidson has sold five during my absence.

Late in 1867, weather being favourable despite the time of year, Davidson decided to make a tour to Berat, which was the northernmost part of his agency. But the weather suddenly changed. As Davidson himself reported it (see the Society's 1868 Report):—

"All night snow had been falling heavily, and when we set out in the morning at daybreak, it was no cheering prospect with six or seven inches of snow on the ground, more falling, and twelve hours before us over a path in nowise good in the summer. About thirty of a caravan started, everyone armed to the teeth with guns, pistols and yataghans. No murders or robberies have occurred for about three years, but the road has such a bad name, that even a mounted policeman will not go alone. We had indeed a bad day of it, sometimes trudging on foot up to the knees in snow; at other times riding, with a cold wind driving the snow in our faces. So cold were the muleteers, accustomed as they were to such hard work, that instead of going forward to the han, they halted after nine hours' journey at the village of Duschari. My hair was frozen to my hat, and I had to sit for a while before I could take it off, when a roaring fire thawed the frost upon our clothes. The village is small and entirely Mohammedan, though of recent conversion from Christianity, possessing a church, but not a single professor of the Christian name."

After a ride of thirteen hours the following day, in somewhat improved weather on the snowy sides of Mount Tomoros, they reached Berat two hours after sunset. Davidson met with a very friendly reception and managed to sell a few copies of the scriptures. Such was the devotion of a man of whom Alexander Thomson wrote that he "never at any time enjoys robust health."

The next town of importance which he visited was Përmet, involving a two-day journey, and no small danger was incurred in fording the swollen rivers. On reaching the town he found all classes so bigoted and ignorant that he effected only one sale. This was partly owing to the fact that the town had, so far as he was aware, never before been visited by any Bible colporteur, and partly owing to orders from the protosingulos[5] of Korçë, which were at once enforced by the same functionary at Përmet. Still the work was begun.

Ill health has always been a hazard to those serving God in Albania, and still is into the 21st century. In February 1868 Thomson from Istanbul:—

---

5 A dignitary in the Greek Orthodox Church.

"I have further to bring the state of matters at Joannina under the notice of the Committee, in connection with the health of Mrs Davidson. For more than a year past, she has been in delicate health, as she was indeed when I saw them last year, but of late things have grown worse... Mr Davidson... feared unless a decided change should take place in Mrs Davidson's health, that ere long he must give notice, as the climate did not seem suitable to her constitution. I think I also intimated to the Committee that Mrs Davidson lost three children, all a few days after birth ... I have uniformly expressed a high sense of the value of Mr Davidson's services, and that I should regret extremely should the Society be deprived of his co-operation, especially after an experience of three years, and a fair practical acquaintance with Modern Greek[6] ... which now make Mr Davidson a much more valuiable labourer than any successor could possibly be for a long time."

The following year's Report observed that Davidson had been unremitting in his efforts to disseminate the Scriptures but encountered "fanaticism and priestly hostility on the one hand, and utter indifference on the other": "and if success has not proved greater, it is to be ascribed to causes which he cannot control, such as the unsettled political state of the province, and the poverty, bigotry, indifference and immorality of the people." Political turbulence prevailed throughout the southern part of his district that year and led to numerous murders and other violence, and a personal trial was also laid upon him by the continued poor health of his wife, yet he performed four important and extensive tours.

Thomson's Report for the year, written in 1868, records a drop in sales, with almost twice as many sales in the north of Albania, where the depot was in Shkodër, as in the south. He adds that "the explanation is simply that in the spring South Albania was disturbed by fears of a Revolution, or of a Greek invasion, so that men's minds were greatly agitated, the wildest rumours were in circulation and travelling in some districts became dangerous, even had people been inclined to purchase the scriptures." Finally, when Davidson was ready and able to set out on a tour, he was prevented by the conduct

---

6 Davidson knew only Greek and a little Turkish, the two cultivated languages of his province; he did not speak Albanian.

of the Pasha, who threw every obstacle in his way. Finally, he set out anyway on his own responsibility, "rather too late for the wild mountain regions through which he passed" as Thomson put it, but in the event he incurred no injury or damage to his health.

Faithfully, Davidson discharged his laborious duties, and Alexander Thomson wrote that "Mr. Davidson had done all that any man could do to promote the circulation of the Scriptures." Low sales were ascribed to the political state of the area, the poverty, the religious bigotry and the indifference of the people themselves. He was chiefly called to witness-bearing for the truth, and scattering the seed among an untaught people; but the Society hoped to see him rejoicing in the conversion of some who had heard his words.

Thomson's 1869 Report says that Davidson performed four extensive tours, including a visit to Delvinë on which:—

"A good many came into the han and read and conversed, but seemed timid. Three of them wished to purchase, but before doing so wished to consult another party who must have been unfavourable, as they did not return.

"In the bazaar an old man got furious at first, when I asked him to buy a New Testament, pouring invectives on both myself and the books, but after a little quiet reasoning he cooled down and spoke friendly, maintaining however that it was a sin for any member of the Orthodox Church to purchase contrary to the instruction of his spiritual guides. He got others to read the Albanian to him, and seemed delighted with it, and from his countenance I thought I saw regret that the books were forbidden. Many admitted to me that they quite believed the Society's editions were correct, but said they could not purchase in the face of the Patriarchal prohibition."

In Vlorë he could neither effect any sales, nor even get into conversation with the people, but it was otherwise at Gjirokastër, where he sold a few copies, and had much conversation. One young lad, who bought an Albanian Testament, was so set on by his companions, that he wished to return it, but ultimately kept it. A merchant also, who had previously purchased the Scriptures, refused to give them up to the priests even though threatened with exclusion from the Lord's Supper.

Mrs Davidson's poor health continued. In the summer of 1869 she stayed for two months with the Thomsons in Istanbul, enjoying the change of air and the company of other Christians, but it brought no decided improvement to her health. She was urged to go back to Edinburgh for at least a year, to benefit as much as possible from a temporary absence from Janinë, and she sailed on 16th June.

In the Bible Society's 1870 Report, Dr Thomson records of Davidson that "nobody could have been more diligent in visiting every part of his wide territory than he has been during the past year." Here are a few glimpses of his three journeys in that Report:—

"The sales were equal to the average of former years, and in some towns they exceeded it considerably; but other places, by the indifference, hostility and mockery with which they treated the Word of God, were a great trial to faith and patience.

"At Parga the people were not so much afraid of the books being bad, as that the priests would demand them and burn them. Where was the use of buying them?

"At Margariti he had to bear much bitterness and rudeness from the youth, but many Moslems came and read the books, while no Christian [i.e. Greek Orthodox] took any notice of them.

"At Gjirokastër, amid much infidelity and indifference, he witnessed the interesting spectacle of the ordination of a priest for the Albanian colonies in the south of Italy."

In Përmet he could sell nothing.

His salary was £90 a year, plus rent and 40% commission on books. On 1st December 1869 Thomson wrote that Davidson had made a ten-week tour, with next to no sales, adding that "I must bear the highest testimony to Mr Davidson's character and work which have procured for him the esteem and respect of all who know him."

By March 1870 Thomson expected Davidson to transfer to Crete the following month or soon after. Before leaving, in April he visited places from Preveza to Gjirokastër. In many places snow still lay thick on the ground and roads were infested with brigands. Everywhere he was received with suspicion: "Your Bibles are good, but they are a preparation for something else." And so his final tour was perhaps the most discouraging of any he had ever made, but he left behind a high reputation for Christian consistency, and his example and conversation had made a contribution to impressing the Word upon some who appeared to have received the truth.

After finishing his duties in Albania, Davidson was transferred to Crete, and a merchant in Ioannina took over the Society's stock. The 1872 Report says that:

> ... during the past year Ioannina, for several years the residence of Mr Davidson, was practically unoccupied, and the whole of South Albania unvisited with the Word of Life. A small depot of Scriptures has been entrusted to a merchant in that city, however, and Mr Tabansky accomplished a visit, which was as successful as could be expected.

By 1873, of Davidson's five children, only one survived: three of the other four had died in Albania. Thomson wrote, "I am satisfied that the three children who died there were a sacrifice to the heartless inhumanity and ignorance of the people among whom Mr Davidson was living—nay of the very nurses that had been engaged."

Another move was proposed: Thomson wished to transfer Davidson from Crete to the island of Chios in July or August 1873. But in the summer of that year, when he was crossing the mountains near Sfakiá in southern Crete, he was seized with pleurisy and was compelled to return to Scotland, where he died in Edinburgh in 1874, aged 38.

Alexander Thomson's Agent's Book for 1873 should perhaps make the final point—and may every reader take it up in prayer and obedient response:

> It is sowing time in these lands, and other labourers besides the colporteur are needed to work them properly. Till such labourers come—and I may say I have appealed for missionaries for Albania, Bosnia and Rumania—I should view the withdrawl of the Society's colporteurs as most disastrous.

"I have appealed for missionaries for Albania." The Albanian Evangelical Mission continues that appeal. Reader, take note, and if God is calling you, count the cost, resolve to pay it, and step forward in acceptance of God's will for your work for Him.

Hermann Riedel

From early in 1864 till 1867, Hermann Riedel was stationed as sub-agent for the Bible Society at Shkodër, and his wife opened a school for girls. The Bible Society's Report for 1865 warned that "owing to the low state of education and the hostility of the Romish clergy, large sales cannot be anticipated."

He experienced hostility from the Roman Catholic clergy; indeed, the Roman and Greek Orthodox church authorities forbade their respective clergy to purchase scriptures from him. After his initial discouragements, Riedel found that interest picked up, and the Turkish Government sent orders to the Pasha of Shkodër that all obstructions to his work should be removed. He visited Pejë, Prizren, Monastir (Bitola), Berat, Vlorë, Elbasan, Durrës and Tiranë. In Tiranë he found a spirit of inquiry among the Moslems, and at Berat even the clergy were favourable to his work. In his first summer, as the Society had as yet no agent in southern Albania, he journeyed as far as Janina and Preveza, suffering much from fever which he experienced again and again in journeys through those beautiful, but often pestilential, districts.

In the Society's Report for 1866 Alexander Thomson reported that Riedel was "of the opinion that among both Moslems and Romanists, but especially the former, there is a considerable amount of religious enquiry ... Mr. Riedel mentions various indications which encourage the hope that the Spirit of God is moving upon the hearts of the people ... In such circumstances, we can only say that it is the duty and privilege of the Society to labour on in faith, and with earnest prayer for the blessing."

The following report appears in the Bible Society's Monthly Reporter for May 1866:—

Enlarged operations.
Among the new spheres of labour upon which the Rev. Dr. Thomson, the Society's Agent for the Turkish Empire, has recently entered, special reference was made in the last Annual Report to Northern Albania, where a suitable centre of operation is established at Scutari [Shkodër], the capital, and from whence other regions are reached with comparative ease. In the course of the past year Mr. Riedel, who acts both as Depositary and Colporteur, undertook extensive journeys for the purpose of circulating the Scriptures in districts greatly needing such Christian efforts. Considering the very limited means of education in many places, combined with much prejudice and gross indifference, the sales effected have proved

satisfactory, and will prepare, it is hoped, for a larger distribution in
future visits. Dr. Thomson alludes in his correspondence to the tours
of Mr. Riedel, and furnishes copious extracts from his interesting
journals:—

I write now for the purpose of giving the Committee some
account of the labours of Mr. Riedel, their Colporteur for the
districts of North Albania, Montenegro and Dalmatia. I need scarcely
inform you that the districts now mentioned are, perhaps without
exception, the most barbarous and spiritually neglected in the whole
Turkish empire. It. will hence create no surprise that our sales have
been, and still are few, while the toils that must be encountered in
effecting them are proportionally greater than almost anywhere else
in Turkey. It gives me great pleasure, in these circumstances, to give
my cordial testimony to the diligence and devotedness of Mr. Riedel,
who has often been obliged to prosecute his labours amid sickness
and weariness, and much discouragement of various kinds. Still he
has not been without some encouragements also ...

I shall now give a short account, derived from Mr. Riedel's letters,
of three journeys which he has recently made, the first being to
Montenegro, and a few other places in Dalmatia ...

Mr. Riedel's next journey was southward from Scutari, through
northern and central Albania, and occupied from June 19th to July
6th. He had visited last year some of the towns in this district, as will
appear from his narrative.

On this occasion I found the roads to some extent insecure, while
the towns are few and far distant; on both of which accounts the
journey was toilsome and. expensive. I first visited Alessia [Lezha], a
small town at the mouth of the Drin, with a Romish monastery on
the opposite side of the river. Here I met with the very lowest grade
of Christianity: among the Turks things are somewhat better. Tiranna
[Tirana] is undoubtedly the most remarkable place in North Albania,
and from thence, I trust, will the Gospel open a path for itself all
around. Thanks be to God for His great grace, that the light has
penetrated into the hearts of these almost heathens. The number of
the enlightened can with difficulty be ascertained, as most of them
are in dependent situations, and in order to retain them, keep silence;
till once a day of the Lord come, when there shall be no more fear,
but men will openly and joyfully confess the Saviour. I think there

are from eight to twelve persons who know and love the truth, and who, if they had any one to instruct them, either in Turkish or Albanian, in the truths of the Gospel, would form themselves into a Christian congregation; and many would soon join them. Among them, there is also a Romanist, named Nicola Gegha, a dyer by trade, with whom I spoke much on the institution of the Lord's Supper. I was happy to find that he had already discarded all fast-days and worship of the saints, and taken for his guide the Bible, which says— "Six days shalt thou labour and do all thy work; and the seventh shalt thou sanctify." Two leading men of this city reside in Constantinople, who are also said to be favourable to the Gospel—Mussulmans of rank. I next reached Ilbassan [Elbasan], where I found the Turks fanatical, and the Greeks domineered over by their Bishop, who required me to repurchase nineteen copies I had sold there last year. I complied, for peace sake, and sold almost the whole of them, in the next town of Berat. This is a pretty large place, and the Greeks seem here somewhat more enlightened than in Ilbassan. I sold many books, especially to the clergy; but the most interesting incident I met with was the following:—

In the han at Berat I met with a company of the wildest-looking men I had ever seen. They were from a place on the banks of the river Lom, and had come with their headman and priest to make purchases in the city. After a few questions, I soon explained to them the object of my journey, and showed them some Testaments. The old Cadi, or Judge, opened the book and examined it for a moment, and then gave it me back with the words—"Have you the Bible, that is, both the Old and New Testament together in one volume? If you have, we would gladly take one with us into our village." I showed them a Bible, and asked twenty-five piastres for it. The priest said he could not examine the book till next day; but that if it was the correct one, they would pay me the money. Next morning, to my delight, the Cadi and priest went away with the book, and brought it back in the evening, accompanied by one or two Mussulmans of rank, to whom the villagers showed much deference. These gentlemen assured them that the Bible contained both Old and New Testament, and was the whole Word of God; upon which the Cadi gave me twenty piastres, and added—"Be assured that, if any of my people visit Scutari, he will pay you the remaining five piastres; for I do not wish to higgle about the book. No! it is a divine book; but we have little money." I reflected hastily—"Who knows how many may be brought to God through this book; and can I withhold it from the inhabitants of a whole district, who thus so earnestly long for it?" I let them have it, and they went their way home, with many wishes for my safety and success. This incident enables us to perceive how many friends of the Truth there are among these heathen Albanians. Oh that there were now a Paul to go from place to place, and rouse them to repentance and faith!

The 1867 Report records four journeys: one to Pejë via Prizren; one to Berat; two to Montenegro. It was believed that the first, the Pejë–Prizren itinerary, was the first occasion on which "those remote and neglected districts" had ever been visited by any missionary or Bible agent. The journey included Gjakova, "chiefly inhabited by Moslems, and bearing the stamp of great poverty and barbarism." Then he went to Deçan by a very dangerous road, and then on to Pejë where he was attacked by a robber who held a gun to his chest and demanded his money. However, Riedel himself was accompanied by a guard who pointed his pistol at the robber and ordered him to give the money back—which he did, and promptly disappeared into the forest. After Pejë, he continued to Guci and Plava, then walked over the mountains for five days back to Shkodër. That itinerary took him from 23rd January till 13th February.

In 1867 Riedel retired from the service of the B&FBS. The the principle reason he assigned was the need of church ordinances for Mrs Riedel and the children. He went to Hungary, and laboured there as a colporteur with fidelity and success under that care of a former colleague of Thomson called Koenig.

He was replaced by Mr. Edward von Laer, who, the following year, made five journeys in Montenegro and Albania, including Prizren where he found the people "disposed, in a degree he had never before witnessed in Albania, to purchase the Scriptures". In 1869 his visits included Durrës, Prishtinë, Prizren, and Manastir. Thomson wrote on 7th September 1969: "At Scutari, we have to face determined and virulent opposition on the part of the Romish clergy and degraded subserviency and superstition on the part of an ignorant populace. But we shall not despair."

Von Laer resigned in 1870 and was replaced by a German, Michael Treiber, who gave himself diligently to the study of the Turkish and Albanian languages. But in Shkodër he found himself "in the midst of a people, few of whom cherish an atom of sympathy for the object which has taken him hither. They are composed mostly of bigoted Romanists and fanatical Moslems." He resigned in 1872.

Thomson looked back longingly to Hermann Riedel, and wrote of him that he had been "our first and best labourer at Scutari ... out of sight the best man we ever had in Scutari". But by 1872 Riedel's wife was suffering from an incurable disease. On the one hand, her health was such that she required a change, and Riedel had written to Thomson to see whether Thomson could employ him again; on the other hand, Thomson wondered whether it would in fact be an advisable move for Riedel to make, as, when Riedel was away on his colportage tours, Mrs Riedel would be almost without a single close friend. "She is an excellent Christian woman and had good influence on the people, but I fear she would find the situation one of hardship for herself." Thomson would have welcomed them back, but it was not to be. 1872 Riedel wrote to Thomson, saying his wife could not at present stand the fatigue of the journey to Shkodër by rail and horseback, otherwise they would both have been willing to come. Thomson took up correspondence with a man called Klundt (who is mentioned earlier in this book) to cover all Albania from Shkodër to Preveza.

When Colporteur Seefried went to Shkodër in 1886, the Roman Catholic clergy declared that whoever listened to, or bought, or read his books denied Christ.

In 1890 the Society reported that "In Scutari, Colporteur Thoshe has done perhaps all that could be expected in that town so difficult to work." The depot closed in 1894.

Clement Sosnovski

Clement Sosnovski was a Bible Society colporteur stationed in Skopje, which currently has an Albanian minority of maybe 100,000 and which is close to the present border with Kosova. His area included places inhabited by Albanians, and in 1880 he crossed the mountains into the disturbed districts held by the Albanian League. He was seen at Prizren in Kosova and was advised to go back. Following this journey, a report was published by the Society in January 1881:—

"A Colporteur was engaged in the summer to work in Macedonia, of whom nothing has now been heard for three months. Dr Thomson writes from Constantinople on December 7:

"I was led by the telegrams received in the course of search for poor Sosnovski to anticipate that he would have been discovered, or have himself returned home by this time. But from a detailed report received, there is great reason to fear that he has, like so many others, fallen a victim to the brigandage that prevails so largely over Macedonia, especially in the north. Mr. Crosbie clings to hope, and thinks his silence for about three months may be accounted for. But I have no such hope, and I greatly fear that the old man himself courted danger by visiting a region that was very unsettled. The last reliable accounts we have of him are, that the Austrian Consul at Uscup [Skopje] saw him at Prisrend [Prizren, Kosova], and counselled him to return to Uscup. It would appear that he engaged horses for Uscup, but as yet no trace of him has been found."

In fact he had hired horses for his return, with his boxes of books, and set out for Skopje on 2nd September 1880.

In a later letter Dr. Thomson reports that he himself was going himself to the neighbourhood in order to assist Sosnovski's wife and children in their trouble, if he should fail to find any clue to the missing man.

Thomson returned to Constantinople on January 5, and sent this account of his journey and its findings:—

I sailed on December 17th, and reached Salonica on the 21st. I at once proceeded to the Rev. P. Crosbie's hospitable residence, and he accompanied me next day to see J. E. Blunt, Esq., H. M. Consul-General. We arranged very thoroughly the further inquiries that seemed desirable. Sosnovski was known to have lodged in the Han kept by one Stephanos, who lets horses on hire and provides drivers.

The Austrian Consul, who saw Sosnovski at Prisrend, and urged him to return to Uscup, informs us that his subalterns assured him they knew for certain that Sosnovski got horses and driver from Stephanos. It seemed right to have this man interrogated whether he had recovered his horses, and what account the driver gave of Sosnovski's disappearance, and that of his two boxes of books, and the clothing with which he had been supplied for a journey expected to last a month.

I proceeded to Uscup by rail on the 23rd, and next day went to the Governor's residence, where I was courteously received by the Kaimakam,7 who really seemed willing to further my inquiries as far as he could. Friday (the Mahomedan Sabbath) being a *dies non,* he invited me to return on the 25th, to have inquiries dispatched by telegraph to the authorities at Prisrend. This I did, and he promised to inform me as soon as an answer should arrive. I did not receive a summons till Tuesday, the 28th, but meanwhile our colporteurs, Klundt and Seefried, arrived, and on clearing their luggage at the Custom House heard that an evasive answer had been received from Prisrend, which was rejected by the Kaimakam as inadmissible.

The reply I did receive was scarcely better. It was to the effect that Stephanos had been summoned to the court, and examined, that he declared that Sosnovski had got horses and driver from someone else, he knew not whom, and he simply knew that be had left for Verisovitch, on the railway, with the intention of going to Pristina [Prishtinë]. As there are only two persons, I am informed, at Prisrend who let out horses, this denial was obviously the result of being afraid to speak the truth and denounce the assassin, lest the life of the witness should be sacrificed to the revenge of the malefactors. Nothing further could be learned through the Government officers. But as Klundt has many intimate friends in that region, he proposed, before returning to Bulgaria, to proceed along the railway to the nearest points to Prisrend, and privately make inquiries among his friends, who must have heard (he is satisfied) of Sosnovski's fate. For that he has been killed nobody doubts. He left Prisrend, as we learn, on September 2nd to return home, whence he had started on August 26th, and since then no trace of him has been found.

---

7 Turkish kaymakàm, governor of an administrative district.

The Austrian Consul was most courteous in affording me all the information he could, and gave it as his opinion that Sosnovski had been shot as a spy by orders of the Albanian League, who rule with despotic sway in Prisrend, Jakova [Gjakovë], and Ipek [Pejë]. That is very probable; but I know, from too many cases in Turkey, that the little money he had with him (under £5), and even his personal clothing and travelling kit, were quite enough to attract the cupidity of a poor and lawless people. But whether by brigands, or by orders of the League, all whom I met at Uscup were satisfied that he must have been killed. Had he died a natural death, there would have been no reason for concealing the fact.

I have reported the result of my inquiries to Consul-General Blunt, of whose ability and zeal shown in this sad affair I cannot speak too highly. I shall wait on the Embassy at Constantinople as soon as possible. Mr Blunt is already in communication with it. Our object now must be to try to procure some small help for the poor widow from the Turkish Government, and to get such affidavits as will satisfy the Austrian Assurance Society of his death, and enable her to procure the sum for which her husband had assured his life. I gave her a small sum to meet immediate wants, till she should be able to find employment of some sort.

Sosnovski had been warned by Klundt not to go to Prisrend, Jakova, or Ipek, which were all in the hands of the Albanian League, and which Klundt had not been able to visit for some years. But the simple old man trusted that his poverty would protect him against robbery, and his quiet unpolitical work against the suspicions of the League, and, knowing that no books had been offered there for sale for some years, he visited Prisrend. He gave me no hint in what direction he meant to make his next tour, else I would have forbidden him by telegraph to go into Albania.

Clement Sosnovski was never seen again. It must be assumed that he lost his life in his efforts to bring the knowledge of God to Kosova.

In addition to such difficulties experienced by Alexander Davidson, Hermann Riedel and Clement Sosnovski, by the early 1880s Albania and Macedonia had been so overrun by brigands that such work could be carried on only at the risk of one's life.

Gjerasim Qiriazi (1858–1894) was the Albanian evangelist who planted the first Evangelical church in Albania, a church which since the fall of Communism has been so signally blessed and has planted daughter churches in a number of surrounding towns and villages. Qiriazi's book, *Captured by Brigands*, tells the story of his six-month captivity at the hands of the notorious brigand Shahin Matraku.

Gjerasim Qiriazi

Qiriazi made the eighteen-hour journey to Korçë in 1884. In the autumn of 1888 he visited Korçë again and was cordially received. He preached repeatedly in the Greek schoolhouse, every room of which was crowded with an attentive audience. The congregations went on increasing, and included Moslems of high position. A deep interest in God's truth was awakened, and Qiriazi was urged to return to Korçë soon. Accordingly, the following year he settled there and had the honour under God of planting the first Evangelical church in Albania in modern times.

It was on his journey from Monastir (Bitola) to Korçë in 1884 that he was captured by brigands—but his own book, translated from Albanian into English by John W. Baird, tells that story, and we merely point our readers' attention to it.

Alexander Thomson wrote of him:

"He had clear and decided views of the great doctrines of the Gospel, and loved to set forth Christ crucified as the power of God and the wisdom of God. But he was especially called to suffer"

This book is offered in the hope that its readers will be stirred to follow the example of those who paid the full price required of them to bring God's light to the Albanian people.

Brigandage in the Ottoman period

Born among Brigands

Mrs Katerina Stefanova Cilka was born in 1870 in Bansko, a small town in what was then known as Macedonia; it is now in Bulgaria. She was Bulgarian by birth, and her husband, Grigor Cilka, was Albanian, born in Korçë in 1875. They had studied at the Congregational mission schools in Monastir (Bitola) and Samakov. Katerina continued her education in America at Northfield Seminary for Girls during the time of the evangelist Dwight L. Moody, and later graduated from the Training School for Nurses of the Presbyterian Hospital in New York City. After serving some time at her profession in America, she was married to Grigor Cilka, who graduated from the Union Theological Seminary in New York. Returning to Turkey, which then included Albania, they began missionary work at Korçë, where Grigor became preacher to the congregation founded by Gjerasim Qiriazi and taught in the girls' school also founded by Qiriazi. Mrs Cilka was an obstetrician and nurse, and devoted some of her time to medical work, in which gained a large influence in the town by her skill and sympathy.

Grigor was both a fervent evangelical preacher and an ardent patriot, supporting wholeheartedly the cause of Albanian independence.

Mihal Grameno, an Albanian patriot who founded the first Albanian-language newspaper in Korçë, wrote that "Cilka was the heart and soul of the national movement, a great and brave man, unwavering though they imprisoned him for this reason." He was imprisoned on several charges in February 1908 and was finally granted an amnesty on 23rd July. In February 1910, he addressed twelve thousand patriots gathered at Korçë for a protest demonstration.

Under war-time conditions, he was the last worker to discontinue his evangelical ministry and escape to Bulgaria.

In the spring of 1901, Grigor and Katerina, and Katerina's friend Ellen Stone, travelled from Korçë to Bansko, where Katerina wished

to visit her parents whom she had not seen for nine years. The
journey, one of the roughest and most at the time in Macedonia,
took them eight days on horseback. In order to enjoy Miss Stone's
company on the journey, the Cilkas delayed their return till 3rd
September, though they had planned to return earlier to Korçë. It
proved to be a momentous decision.

But Mrs Cilka, together with Miss Stone, was taken captive by
Macedonian brigands. She told her story in *McClure's Magazine*, Vol.
19, #4 (August 1902):

IT WAS A WINTER NIGHT, the 3rd of January, 1902. The sky was
beautiful and bright with a myriad of twinkling stars. Gigantic
mountains towered on both sides of a mountain path which wound
itself along a murmuring brook.

A mysterious party was moving cautiously and rapidly along the
narrow trail. Three men in single file, about sixty or seventy feet
ahead, watched for any danger, ready to signal for retreat if necessary.
Four or five men followed, then two horses, whose riders were
carefully wrapped in long black *kepes* (mountaineer coats of padded
goats' hair). Heavy hoods covered their heads, hiding half of their
faces. Each horse was led by a guard. On each side of both riders also
marched other guards holding fast to their saddles. This was to
protect the riders from unexpected falls. Close behind the horses
more men followed, and then about 90 or 100 feet behind was the
rear-guard, consisting of two or three men. There were also a
number of scouts who, shadow-like, appeared and disappeared
among the trees. The whole party, except the scouts, moved in single
file. They wore black *kepes*. Daggers hung from their belts. Each man
had a revolver on his left, and a loaded gun, firmly held in his right
hand. Cartridge belts crossed their breasts and surrounded their
waists. Their steps were light. Only their heavy breathing was heard
as they climbed the mountain side. No talk, no coughing, no
sneezing was allowed. The dead silence was occasionally broken by
the clink of some dagger hitting against a gun. Now and then a
whistle was heard, a signal at which every man instantly took
position to fire; but, thank God, there was no occasion for firing that

night. This peculiar party moved on and on for ten hours. Suddenly it halted in a ravine The riders dismounted and sat down, while the others proceeded to smoke cigarettes. One of these riders was Miss Ellen M. Stone, captured on the 3rd of September, and dragged through the mountains in this fashion, now exactly four months. The second rider was myself, her companion in misery. The armed men were, of course, the brigands who caught us.

After a few moments' rest, the signal was given to proceed, the journey now being no longer by a path, but up the untraveled mountain side, over shrubs and thorns and stones. We had to climb on foot, for it was impossible to hold on in the saddle. For me, walking was not to be thought of: how could it be expected of a woman who was awaiting the advent of her little one any day or night, and who had traveled ten hours in the wintry cold night on the rough mountains? Now for the first time I had no fear of the brigands, for they could do nothing worse than kill me, and I cared not whether I lived or died. When they ordered us to climb I sat down and refused to move.

"Go," I said, "and leave me here to die in peace. It is wicked and outrageous to drive about a woman in my condition."

Two strong arms lifted me and dragged me up the fearful mountain side. I had no strength to speak or cry, I had no hope left. After a time, I do not know how long, we reached a peculiar little hut among trees and rocks.

Two or three men inspected it cautiously, and finding it deserted, forced the door open. Miss Stone and I sat down outside until they were ready to ask us in. The hut was constructed on an elevation projecting between two lofty mountains. Streamlets of water oozed out from the cracks of the rocks. The ground was covered with heavy frost; it was very cold. Soon a blazing fire from the hut reflected itself on the opposite mountain side. Now we were motioned to enter. My feet were numb with cold, but I was suffering so much with the pain of fatigue that I did not sit near the fire to get warm. I looked for a place to lie down and rest my aching back. In a corner near the fire some straw was spread. A log was given me for a pillow. A *kepe* was then spread over the straw, and this was to be my bed. I lay down half-dead with exhaustion and pain. Miss Stone sat near the fire and talked with the brigands, who were drying their foot wrappings, and then she lay down beside me. They stretched themselves every which way on the part of the floor not occupied by us. Only one stood guard. The fire burned brightly, the smoke floated like a cloud around the room, and found its way out through the cracks, for there was no chimney. The men slept and snored heavily. I turned and twisted, but no position was comfortable. I sat up in bed and looked around. Four stone walls and a thatched roof shining with soot inclosed the little room. On either side stood two tremendous wine casks. One was old and broken, the other smelled of fresh wine. A small wooden tub and a gourd stood near at hand. These were all the belongings of our hut. The smoke blinded my eyes, and the tears began to run down my cheeks. I wished there was a chimney, for the smoke was oppressive. How the brigands did snore! I looked at Miss Stone, lying close by my side. She was sound asleep. Her pretty, small hands were laid one on top of the other, under her cheek; they were black with dust and smoke. I smiled as I looked at her, but my smile soon disappeared, for a fearful pain shot through my back. Again I turned and looked at Miss Stone; I both pitied and envied her. "She is tired, but she can sleep at least." A pair of black eyes attracted my attention. The guard was closely watching me from his dark corner. I became nervous and turned my back to him.

"Why don't you sleep?" Miss Stone said. "Lie down, childie."

I did so, but another pain, worse than the previous, forced me to get up again. I thought I was too tired to rest. "That wretched saddle nearly broke my back last night," I said. Miss Stone went sound asleep again. The men snored as usual, the guards changed.

Some one pushed the door open, and to my surprise it was daylight. Presently the brigands began to stir. Some got up, sat around the fire, opened their knapsacks, and proceeded to breakfast on dry bread and cheese. Others slept on. Those who finished breakfasting went to sleep again.

Now it was some time after midday. All were asleep again except the guard. I was getting more and more miserable. The guard turned and looked at me thoughtfully, then stepped near the chief brigand and whispered something in his ear.

He at once sat up, rubbed his eyes, looked toward me, and finally addressed me

"Madam, you had better lie down and sleep; to-night we have a long journey to make."

I broke into tears and sobs.

"How can I travel? My hour has come! What will become of my dear baby? They will kill it as soon as it comes into the world."

At this Miss Stone wakened.

"Why do you cry, childie?"

No answer was necessary. She understood it all. She turned and spoke to the chief. She said it was impossible for me to travel that night.

"We must," he said. "We must leave this place; it is dangerous."

"Kill me if you wish it, but I do not move from this hut to-night. If I die, let me die here and not on the road," I said.

He again lay down, but not to sleep. He became anxious; he twisted and turned and watched me closely. His heart was touched. He was human, after all.

"If madam wishes, we shall all go out and leave you alone," he said somewhat gently.

"Yes," I said very quickly and positively.

He then touched each man, until they all were sitting up rubbing their eyes, trying to awaken and see what was going on.

"Hasten," he said. The men were on their feet and at once disappeared. Miss Stone and I were left alone.

The hours dragged slowly. My agony was intolerable. Miss Stone was getting more and more nervous. She dreaded my fate. No bed, no clothes, no convenience of any kind, not even water. Fire was all we had, but in spite of it the room was very cold, for there were big open spaces all around the thatched roof.

I had on two thick pairs of stockings and heavy boots, but still my feet were cold.

"No," I said, "I shall never pull through. If I survive the pain, the cold will kill me."

Then I decided to leave my message to my husband and mother. I asked Miss Stone to give my engagement and wedding rings to my husband, and tell him how dearly I loved them in this four months. My heart ached with pain when I thought of their sorrow and grief for me, and especially when they should hear that I had died under such circumstances.

A gentle hand touched the door. A woman! What a surprise. We had longed to see a woman for the last four months. How happy we both were to see one again. A woman! Evidently the brigands had taken her from some hut, and against her will brought her to us for the emergency. She was an old woman, perhaps fifty or sixty years of age. Her face was pleasant, her features regular, though lacking intelligence. It was difficult to ascertain what race she belonged to, for she was black with smoke and dirt. The space between her heavy wrinkles were embedded with dirt, accumulated there for months, and perhaps years. The gray hair hung loosely over her forehead and eyebrows. Her head was covered with a kerchief which had been white once upon a time. She also wore a black garment so patched that there was very little left of the original. Half of a sleeve and the collar were entirely gone. Her feet were bare and chapped from the cold and exposure. She looked at us with great surprise and reverence. Our ways and clothes were a mystery to her. She looked at us as if to say, "What creatures these mortals be!" She had never seen other people outside her family. The poor woman appeared frightened by the brigands, who had strongly forbidden her to talk to us on any subject, except concerning the one thing for which she was brought to us. The first thing she did was to fetch a dish of water. She asked me in the most matter-of-fact way to drink some of the water, and also to be sprinkled with it.

"Do," she said. "It is sacred water." I, however, refused very politely. Failing in her first attempt to bring relief, she then produced a tin box, in which she wished me to blow *very hard*. I laughed in spite of my trouble. She was a good little woman. I asked her to sit by the fire and rest, and told her that when I needed her I would call for her.

Now it was twilight; silence reigned, broken only by the whistling of the wind and the slow steps of the guard outside. The fire was blazing, the wood crackled as the heat approached it. The back of the room was in shadow and darkness. At the farther end of the fire sat the good old woman, nursing her knees and shaking her head as a sign of approaching calamity. Miss Stone sat on a log opposite the woman. She kept the fire going and prayed in her heart. Her face was sad, but full of "blessed assurance." She had on her head a dark kerchief as a protection from both the cold and the soot which fell from the roof. Her garments, of a dark, coarse homespun, had been sewn by her own fingers. I often heard her say, "Childie, what can I do to help you?" but there was nothing with which to do anything. We had no medicine, not even a hot drink of any kind.

I was standing now with both hands tightly clutched at the rings of the wine cask. My strength was gone, and yet there was no one to help me.

The thought passed my mind like a flash: "Where is my mother? Where is my husband? Why am I so far from my dear ones? Oh, so far, I do not know how far! They certainly think of me. They grieve for the lost one. Oh, mother, where are you? Oh, God, help me!" The pain, aggravated by the previous night's long and rough ride, was intolerable. I wished for rest, I wanted death, for to die is to rest from all suffering. "Pray for me, Miss Stone," I cried.

At 10 p.m. all was over. Both women were alive with excitement. The old woman was wrapping the crying infant, for we had been able to make a few simple clothes for the little one. During the first months of our captivity we felt as though we should go insane from idleness. Finally Miss Stone suggested that we ask the chief for some material out of which to be making baby's dresses. He consented to give us what they had—ten yards of cheese cloth, and about six yards of heavy white woolen homespun cloth. The gauze they used for the purpose of cleaning their weapons, and the heavy cloth for foot wrappings. We were both as happy as children over these materials, and proceeded at once to cut out the garments. They supplied us with thread and needles, even with thimbles. Out of the cheese cloth we made shirts and dresses for baby. The dresses had five or six tucks at the bottom, all hemstitched and featherstitched. The shirts were made the same way. Out of the coarse cloth I cut blankets for baby and hemstitched them all around and it the middle. All the feather-stitching was done with heavy white spool thread. We took very short stitches, in order to get as much work out of it as possible. When all the ends and seams were feather-stitched, we began over again making new rows of feather-stitching. In such wonderful garments we dressed my baby when it was born.

Now while the old woman was at work Miss Stone stood smiling, chattering and repeating over and over again, "Blessed girl, blessed girl, it is a blessed girl!" putting the emphasis on "blessed." She certainly was a blessing to us during the long, dreary hours afterwards. The old *baba* (midwife), with an air of pride and satisfaction, was squatted near the fire warming the newcomer.

"You must have some kind of hot drink," said Miss Stone, "but there is nothing to make it of."

Finally we thought of barley. The brigands had some for their horses. We could cook it, and it would be a nice drink. The brigands brought an old black copper kettle. They hung the handle on a green stick, and rested the two ends of the stick on two high stones on each side of the fire. Our barley cooked quickly, and soon I had a nice hot drink. We found it so good that it became the fashion among the brigands afterwards. They liked it very much; besides it was so cheap and easy to get.

My baby was still crying; it had not yet recovered from the cold shock.

My poor baby! My darling, what is to become of you? Will these men spare you when you disobey their "Sht! Keep still!" Babies and their cries are the sweetest charm in the world, but the most undesirable things among brigands.

"Where are they?" I thought. "They must be holding council somewhere as to how to take away my poor baby."

The door was pushed open. The youngest brigand walked in. He looked somewhat shy.

"Is it a boy?" he asked.

"A blessed girl," was Miss Stone's quick answer.

He frowned. I thought I understood why he frowned.

A knife passed through my heart, as we say in Bulgaria.

"Well," he said, "if it were a boy, we would make a brigand of him, but a girl does not make a good brigand, although there are stories told of girls who became *voivodi* (leaders of brigands)." He hesitated a little and said: "I don't know, after all, we may make her the daughter of the *cheta* (band)."

After a few more similar remarks he picked up the gourd, filled it with wine which he drew from the wine cask at my heal, spattering some of the wine in my face as he drew it, for the faucet was near my head, and started for the door with the words, "I shall take this wine to the *cheta*. We must drink the health of the little brigand." Poor excuse for a drink!

Two or three hours later the chief himself appeared. He was tall, heavily built, and dark. His eyes were fierce at other times, but now they were downcast. He said nothing; he stood in front of the fire and seemed deep in thought. Every time the baby cried or grunted he was startled; he was not used to that sort of thing. Everybody in the room way silent except the baby. To break the oppressive silence Miss Stone picked up the infant and handed it to the chief (this is just like Miss Stone). At first he appeared confused and embarrassed, but as he watched the little helpless morsel in his strong arms a smile passed over his face. I was anxious, I watched his expression, I read his thoughts, I waited for results. And, sure enough, his smiles lasted longer, he bent his head closer to baby's face. He was no more a brigand to me, but a brother, a father, a protector to my baby. He now made up his mind to have a good time, so he sat down by the fire and began to warm baby's feet. My heart jumped with joy, I was relieved.

"He means to spare my child. He can do it, he is the chief." His voice was deep and somewhat melodious, and now it was the sweetest music in my ears, for he spoke of baby; he was concerned that the baby should not catch cold. He sprang to his feet, gave the infant back to Miss Stone, and asked her for a list of things necessary for the mother in the line of food.

"I shall give these orders and shall soon return."

True to his word, he came back again.

"Now," he said, addressing Miss Stone and the old woman, "you lie down to sleep. As for baby, I shall sit down here and keep her warm."

The old *baba* lay down on the ground and soon began to breathe heavily. She felt quite at home, for her home was no better than our hut. Miss Stone, like a heroine, did all she could to make me warm and comfortable, and then lay down on the bare earth near my feet. She soon fell asleep, for she was very tired. As for me, sleep did not seem to come. I was watching my baby. I wanted to know its fate during the night, but I must have fallen asleep, for I jumped up frightened. "Where is baby?" I whispered to myself

I looked around the room. The two women were asleep. The chief sat near the fire with his back turned to me, and his head nodding with sleep. Baby was sweetly resting in this man's strong arms. I looked at him. I examined him well. There was the revolver on his side, there the fatal dagger, and there, too, the little baby gently cuddled in those iron-like arms. I both smiled and wept with joy. I thanked God for the gentleness in this man.

Is it possible? Is this the same man I saw only a few months ago so mercilessly stabbing a poor victim to death?

Is he the same man who not long ago bragged and threatened our lives? Yes, he is the very same. Who wrought this change in him? Nobody but the little wee baby. Morning came, the chief was no longer shy. He patronized the baby. He called her by many pet names. She was "the little brigand, the daughter of the *cheta*," but his favorite was Kasmetche (good luck). He did all he could to make us happy and comfortable. He kept the fire going, he boiled barley, cooked chicken, and made himself as useful as he could. This same man forgot all about danger outside. This little wee thing had stolen his heart. He was thinking and talking of nothing else but of the little Kasmetche. He laughed, he joked, he appeared as happy as though it were his own baby.

Now we were treated more like free people and not as captives; that is, we were spoken to.

The *voivoda* (chief) now asked me if the rest of the men could come to see the baby and congratulate me. Of course I was only too glad to have them come, and see what they would say, how they would act. It was dark now. We made no preparations for the reception. We had no lamps to trim, no refreshments to serve, no chairs to arrange. The party of brigands came unannounced. Most of them were tall, striking fellows. Each one as he entered shook hands with me, congratulated me, and stood back so as to make room for the others. The rest followed in the same way until there were two long rows of fully armed men crowded into the little room. They rested on their guns, gazed at the blazing fire, and made some pretty speeches while baby was passed from man to man. In a corner behind them stood timidly the good old *baba*. Miss Stone was the queen of the occasion. She talked to them, she laughed with them, she made them feel perfectly at home. The mother was radiant; she forgot that she lay in straw, she only thought that her baby was safe. What a picture! What a reception! Are these brigands and these captives? What a transformation, all because of a baby! The brigands appeared very jolly. One said that they must give baby presents. He himself offered to make her a pair of sandals. Another one said he would make her a whistle, and the chief offered to make her a brigand's outfit.

"What are you going to call her?" one asked.

"Ellena," I said, "in honor of my mother and of Miss Ellen M. Stone."

"Do you know," said another, "no *cheta* has ever had a baby born among them. This is an extraordinary event for us. We shall immortalize her name. It shall be written on our guns. Ellena shall be written on our guns."

Another brigand spoke out: "This mother makes me think of Mary, the mother of Christ. She, too, lay in straw, and it was about this time of the year."

"No," said another, "this is a martyr; no woman has suffered as she has."

Then they all turned and looked at me with great pity. After giving baby a hearty kiss they bade us good-night and disappeared out in the darkness. I believe they had a great discussion that night, whether it was wise to preserve the life of the newcomer or not.

It was the second day after baby's birth. The sunbeams peeped in the hut through the many cracks and holes. Two brigands were with us now, both to guard and to wait on us.

One was stretched along the fire, and the other sat against the door. The room was dark as in the night, except for the sun's rays that crept through the holes. The smoky roof and the many spider webs became monotonous to my eye; I longed for light, for sunshine. The sunshine is so near and yet so far. It is outside the door. If they would only open the door just a little bit. It seemed to me as if I should go insane in such darkness. I became nervous, desperate.

"Please open that door, I want to see the sunshine. Nobody can see us in this mountain."

"Oh, yes," they said, "only it is very cold."

They opened the door, and there was the glorious sunshine, there the mountain side with dry, brown oak leaves. I was feasting now on a small patch of nature's beauty, and it was so sweet. The chief walked in.

"We shall have to travel to-night," he said. "It is very unsafe here, but do not worry. We shall make you very comfortable for the journey. We shall carry you in a box, and as for the baby, one of us will carry it. They will begin to make the box very soon."

Of course all I had to say was, "Very well."

The men as well as Miss Stone were making preparations for the journey. "Klink, klink" was heard outside. The box was being made of planks. Toward night the weather changed. It became chilly, and soon the snow was falling very rapidly. My good old *baba* had been home and returned to bid us good-by and give her present to baby. The present consisted of a dark red cap decorated with one silver coin and a piece of garlic. The garlic is used as a preventive against evil eye. She also gave baby a plaid handkerchief, such as you see among the working Italians. After spitting on her finger and placing it in baby's mouth, she took her departure. As the evening approached fears began to creep into my heart. I was not able to turn on my side as yet; even my cough caused me great pain. How am I to stand a whole night's jarring on a box on horseback? And poor baby, how is she going to nurse?

Miss Stone was asked to get everything ready. Very soon we heard much talking outside. All the brigands were together discussing the question, whether the horses were strong enough to carry such heavy loads, especially my horse. Finally a long wooden box, just like a coffin, was brought into the hut. It suggested death, and I was to be the corpse. My eyes filled with tears. Many men came in to see how I was to be placed in it. I became indignant. "Go out," I said. "Only two men are necessary to place me in it."

The bottom of the box was spread with a rug of ours, and a half of an old dirty quilt. I was then lifted by two men and placed in it, and then covered with the other half of the quilt. One of the brigands tried to lift the box, but it was very heavy. "Useless," he said. "It is too heavy. This horse is not strong enough. It will drop somewhere on the road, and then—" he looked questioningly.

Many rushed in to see what was the trouble. They all tried lifting me, and all came to the same conclusion, that it was too heavy.

"What is to be done? The potera (pursuers, soldiers) are in search of us. They are not far from us."

"We must fly," said the chief, "or else we are all lost."

They again turned their faces toward the box. I was the obstacle. They did not know what to do with me, how to dispose of me. I covered my face and wept aloud in the box. The chief again glanced at me and spoke.

"Well, we shall have to leave her here with one of us, and let both be disguised in peasant's clothes. If the army find them they will take them for villagers living here. And now, Miss," turning to Miss Stone, "you must come with us."

I never shall forget the shock and expression on Miss Stone's face. She was both frightened and indignant.

"No," she said, "I don't part from Gospoja (the Mrs.)."

The sight was tragic. I shall never forget how two of the brigands, the youngest, stood for us. They said: "We shall stay here one more night. If danger comes we shall fight, even if we die. To-morrow we send for strong horses, make the box lighter, and Gospoja will be better able to travel by to-morrow night."

All agreed. I was taken out of the box and again placed on my old straw. That night both Miss Stone and I wept, we felt so badly. Baby cried, too. The next day was spent in the same way as the day before. Night came again. Strong horses were brought, and my box was made shorter, which reduced its weight considerably. Baby was prepared for the journey in the following way. Next to the skin she had a gauze shirt. A napkin was wrapped around her thighs and legs. Then a layer of cotton on top of that. Thick woolen cloth was used to keep her feet warm and well protected. Several woolen blankets were used in wrapping her from neck to feet. Her hands were tied down by her side next to her shirt. Over all these a big blanket was wrapped around her, one corner projecting so as to fall over the head and protect it from the wind and snow. She had on the cap which the *baba* gave her. One of the brigands came into the hut and rehearsed his part in carrying baby. I suggested that he had better give his gun to somebody else to carry. "No," he said, "if I lose my gun I may lose both baby and myself." I felt uneasy to have them carry baby. I still feared that they might choke her if she cried at some dangerous place. Miss Stone understood my feelings, and offered herself to carry the baby. Some kind of sling was prepared for the purpose, a square piece of cloth with a string on each corner. Baby was placed in it, and then the strings were tied around Miss Stone's neck and waist. It hung something like a hammock in front of her. Four pieces of sugar were tied in four different places in a thin cloth for baby to suck on the way whenever she cried. Now all was ready. I was again placed in the box, and four men took me out of the hut to the horse and at once began loading the poor animal. The box with me in it was fastened on one side of the clumsy saddle, and the other side had to be balanced with logs of wood and stones. It was a very heavy and bulky load. My horse was started while Miss Stone and baby were being fixed. As the path was very narrow and steep the box began to slide back and almost drag on the ground. I felt it did not balance well, but it was so dark that the men could not see. The horse was excited and climbed very fast, the men could hardly control it. I heard them say, "Hold on the box, it is going to upset. It is going down the hill. Hold on, hold on!" Crash went the box against a tree. I felt as though my brains were knocked out. Five or six men grouped like bees around my horse and prevented an accident. We proceeded again on the rough journey, the box hitting here against a tree, there against a stone, and many times I fell on the ground as the horse stumbled. I thought that if I were a little stronger I would get out and walk, but such a thing was impossible. I was so tortured and frightened that I could not even cry. In the hands of brigands this cold night, they may soon get tired of me and throw me down into some river or over a precipice. Yes, in the hands of men who care nothing about me. And there is baby crying. O Misery, where is thy end? My baby, my precious darling, you are cold and hungry, but your mother is tightly strapped in a box; she can't come to you, she dare not speak. The poor thing had sucked all the sugar we had for her, now she was crying very hard.

"Oh, please, please," I broke into tears, "give me my baby. Let me nurse it. It will die!" No answer came. "Please, I want to see the chief." No answer again, although the men were near my horse. Miss Stone's horse was much ahead, so that I could not hear baby's cry distinctly, but mothers' ears are sharp. I heard the pathetic cry of my darling. "Oh, God, my heart will burst!" From where I got strength I do not know, but I pushed at the ropes tied around the box, and raised myself in a sitting position. It was blowing and snowing, and the men rushed to me and ordered me to lie down and cover myself. I was defiant. "My baby please. Oh, give it to me. I can nurse it here. O Chief, please, please give me my baby."

My wish at last was granted. I seized the little ball (it looked like a ball) and pressed her to my heart. She appeared as if she understood it all. She nursed, and she sobbed. Only three days in the world and so much trouble!. While I was nursing her two or three brigands took their *kepes* off their backs, hung them on their guns, and made something like a tent around us. Baby was again taken to Miss Stone. I lay in the box, and the journey proceeded. Now we had traveled seven hours. My horse was so tired that he made several attempts to lie down.

"Drive," said the chief to the brigands. "Don't let the horse lie down. We are lost if this horse gives out."

The journey went on over stones, rocks, and steep hillsides, and the men were tired, they could not krepi (support) my horse; they began to linger behind in spite of the chief's haida (hasten). Dawn was breaking. We all had to hide before it was daylight. Another gigantic effort by both men and horses, and the destination was reached. My face was covered as I lay in the box. I felt the ropes being unfastened. Many hands were lifting and carrying the box. I felt as though it was passed through a narrow door and then through another one, and with a jerk the box landed on the ground. My face was uncovered, and I found myself in a room similar to our previous one, except for the wine casks. We had the same kind of walls and roof and no chimney. We did not know when it was day and when night; it was always dark. Baby cried a good deal when we arrived here. I had no strength to amuse it. Miss Stone was sitting near the fire and singing baby to sleep (in whispering tone).

"Oh," she said, "if I only had a rocking chair, how I would put this baby to sleep."

I laughed, for it struck me very funny to be thinking of a rocking-chair when we did not have even the simplest stool to sit on. Here I had chills and fever the first day, but the next day I was well again (comparatively speaking). After two days we had to run away again, for the potera were upon us. To carry me in a box was too much trouble for the men. They filled two bags of straw, fastened them on either side of the saddle, and I rode on top of those. The journey was short this time, about two hours. From now on our journeys were shorter; we simply moved from place to place.

Now it was a month since baby was born. We were in a miserably cold and smoky hut. Miss Stone and I had bad colds and coughed incessantly. Baby coughed, too. The tears were running down our cheeks from the smoke and also from the cough. We were lying down to sleep. The room was full of brigands, and the odor was very bad. That night I cried bitterly. It seemed as if I could not endure it any longer. A man stepped near us and threw a letter to Miss Stone, which she at once proceeded to read. I could not wait to have it read.

"Is the money paid?" I asked excitedly.

"Yes," said one of the brigands.

The happiness we felt was too great to be expressed in words.

Ellen Stone continues the story in McClure's Magazine:

Only two horses were provided for that night's journey, so Mrs Tsilka and I carried the baby by turns. It was hard to believe that it could be true that we were to be freed. The whole band started with us—the guard before, the guard behind, and scouts deploying upon either side. Thus we traveled for an hour, when there seemed to be one of those strange alarms which had soon often been a feature of our nightly experiences. Some of the men threw themselves upon the ground; others drew off to one side for consultation. Were they to be attacked, and we ourselves to be killed, now that our freedom seemed so near? Then we heard the cautious words, "Let the horses start."

The path began to descend steeply, and before we could realize that the rest of the band were no longer with us, we had gone too far to see any of them save the two who remained to guard us. So quickly and unexpectedly had come our deliverance. For six hours more our journey continued. Finally, at about ten o'clock Turkish, or four o'clock on Sabbath morning, the 23rd, we had descended the last of the foothills, we had crossed the last of the mountain streams, and we found ourselves upon a plain. The brigands dismounted us under a pear tree, and told us to sit there until daylight. "Then," they said, "you can get some passer-by to help you carry the saddle-bags and your pillows into the village."

... It was a clear, sunny, glorious morning, and we enjoyed unspeakably the sense of freedom to rejoice in its brightness, and to journey at our own sweet wills. After a little rest and light refreshments at a Turkish guard-house on the top of the mountain, there was a glad surprise for us, but most of all for Mrs Tsilka. Two young men were approaching with long, gladsome steps. She did not see them until her husband came beside her. Over that blessed meeting between the long-separated and long-suffering husband and wife, and the first meeting of that father with his daughter, we may well draw a veil. Mrs Tsilka had been terribly cast down by a rumor that when we were released her husband would be thrown into prison. In vain we tried to persuade her that it could not be so. She had refused to be comforted; but here now was the husband, walking by the side of her horse, and carrying his daughter in his arms.

Grigor Cilka fell victim to influenza in late 1918 when he was in Sofia, and died there early the following year. Edwin Jacques wrote that his wife lived in Tirana and survived the Second World War. She died in 1950 in Tirana.

Elena (Elenche) Cilka grew up and went to Robert College in Istanbul, but as she emerged from adolescence she developed tuberculosis. Towards the end of her short life she fell in love with George Minor, a young American working for the American Legation in Tirana and married him, but she and died in Istanbul in 1925.

Grigor Cilka and his daughter

Her brother Skender graduated from Cornell University in the United States and returned to Albania. In 1948, it was reported that he had been sentenced to ten years imprisonment. He died in Albania in 1974.

Note: An Internet search on Katerina, Elena and Skender produce slight discrepancies concerning the dates and places of their deaths. I have used those provided by Dr Richard Cochran, Dean of Library, Ferris State University, Big Rapids, Michigan, Katerina's great grandnephew.—David Young

The Evangelical church, Korçë

AEM's book *Battle for Albania* (1998, now out of print) gives the story of the spiritual awakening in Korçë in the late 1930s, as we learnt it from Edwin Jacques, who was an American Baptist missionary in Korçë from 1932 till 1940. What follows is an enlarged version of that story and of its continuation during the Second World War and the Communist period.

Prelude:
British and Foreign Bible Society Depot

Thanas Sina, the Bible reviser, was born near Leskovik in 1859. Whilst serving as a colporteur for the British and Foreign Bible Society he was arrested in Berat in 1903 and all his books were seized. He was deported to his native village where the whole population were required to stand guarantee for him. His house was ransacked and all his private papers were taken away. Following the death on 30th December 1913 of Gjergj Qiriazi, brother of Gjerasim Qirizai, he took charge of the Bible Society depot in Monastir (Bitola), which was transferred to Korça in 1921. He also taught at the boys' school in Korçë, and became superintendent of the Bible Society depot in Korçë. In 1925 completed his translation of the Old Testament into Albanian. He retired due to poor health on 1st March 1925, and a fortnight later was seized with a stroke and confined to bed for a period. He died in 1934.

The next Superintendent at Korça was Loni Kristo, who married Efthimia, the daughter of Thanas Sina. He was educated at Harvard and Princeton and came to Korçë as head of English at the Korçë lycée. He often came to the Evangelical mission, and formed a close friendship with Phineas Kennedy, American missionry in Korçë from 1908. He also completed the translation of the Old Testament. In the first year of the Italian occupation (April 1939 to March

1940) 2,925 copies of the Scriptures were circulated, representing a slight increase over the previous year; most were from the depot under Loni Kristo, and 922 were circulated by Thanas Sina's son, colporteur Pandeli Sina, who had previously been a village schoolteacher. Because of Loni Kristo's American sympathies the Italians arrested him in 1941 for anti-fascism, and sent him to an internment camp on the island of Ischia in the bay of Naples. He never returned to Korçë, and he and his wife did not become involved with the Communists. Eventually they retired and both died in 1960.

Thanas Sina

The depot was in the basement of a house belonging to Thanas Mborja. From 1947 there was no director, but the books remained in the basement, unavailable, or bought only with difficulty.

Sometime in the period 1964-8, the Communists took all remaining New Testaments and other literature from the depot and either burnt it or made it into pulp for carton containers for sugar, rice and so on. Thousands of New Testaments were destroyed in this way.

The Church: the Awakening

Koci Treska

Koci Treska was born on 2nd February 1913 in Treska, a mainly Orthodox village; his father was a trader, with a shop in the village

Koci Treska

of Panarit. His uncle Sotir Treska wrote an article in the magazine "Ylli i Mëngjezit" in 1917 or 1918 (published in Worcester, Mass.), under the title "Zjarri në Toskëri". The article tells how Koci's father was burned alive by the Greeks in 1914, in a house with two others. "Ylli i Mëngjezit" was edited by Parashqevi Qiriazi (1880-1970), Gjerasim's sister, from her temporary home in Worcester, Massachusetts, from January 1917 till 1920.

In 1916 the survivors of Treska all moved to Korçë. Koci's mother worked with rugs.

Koci went to American missionary Phineas Kennedy out of school hours for lessons in English, and was converted in about 1927 or 1928. He was a gentle and meditative character.

He graduated from the local lycée in 1937 with a bachelor's degree in philosophy. Having been very helpful in translation work, he sensed a call to Christian service. His lycée instruction having been in the French language, he applied to the Institut Biblique in the Paris suburb of Nogent sur Marne. They arranged a work scholarship for him. One year of kitchen work, with some mission assistance, would support him through the two-year Bible course. Materialistic acquaintances would charge him with "changing his religion for a scholarship abroad". Certainly they would do just about anything to study in Paris; but they could never imagine washing dishes or peeling potatoes. No scholar would do that! But Koci would.

He remained unmoved by his uncle's tirade: Your mother lost her patriot husband twenty-four years ago; now she loses her son! As for you, go! A pleasant journey! But never call me 'Uncle'; never call her 'Mother'. You shame the living and the dead.

All the many formalities were completed, outfit collected, suitcase packed, bus, boat and railway reservations made.

But just one hour before bus departure, the fanatical mother and relatives and neighbours staged such a hysterical demonstration that he had to stay at home. She prostrated herself on the steps, grovelling and writhing and screaming that if he stepped over her body to leave for Paris, she would kill herself. And certainly she would have done just that.

Training

Nor was that the end of it. The following February (1938), a high-level delegation of two professors and a high dignitary spent three hours urging the missionaries to prohibit Koci from attending mission functions. "They warned us that we could expect to 'lose prestige, to say the least'!"

That summer while walking back from an afternoon meeting in a mountain village, a small group emerged from a gorge and rounded a shoulder of the mountain as the sunlight faded. It was a breathtaking sight—with the blue smoke from thousands of supper fires hanging like a halo over each of the many villages scattered across the broad Korça plain. On the spot, two of the young men, a tinsmith and a shoemaker, determined to quit their jobs at once and do commit themselves to the work. So on 1st. August 1938 the missionaries felt constrained to improvise a home-made Bible Institute for their training. Three young men came to the mission each morning for three hours of study in the Acts of the Apostles. Each afternoon they went out to threshing floors and farms surrounding Korça, distributing tracts and selling the Scriptures. To enable them to care for dependent families, the mission provided a small supplement to the Bible Society commission on Scripture sales.

Following two weeks of Biblical instruction and practical experience, the young men had two weeks to go back into the more remote villages. Their primary purpose was colportage work, but opportunities came for meetings with children and women during the afternoon, and with men during the evening. They returned with stirring accounts of crowded gatherings and a warm reception.

Thus the foreign missionaries felt catapulted by circumstances into a programme for training workers as mission helpers so as to reach the many villages systematically.

The combined classes and colportage continued for five weeks. These three and another who had completed the Christian Life class asked for baptism. The date was set for Sunday, 11th September.

Nikolla Çeno

Stojna Çeno had been converted in Manastir, under the ministry of Mrs Kennedy's father-in-law, the Rev. Lewis Bond, who maintained a mission school in Manastir. She had been a helper to the Bond family. Her son Nikolla was brought up in Korça and graduated from an agricultural school in Greece maintained by the American Board of Commissioners for Foreign Missions. Later, before the War, he studied at the Bible School in Villach, Austria, which was established in 1922 to prepare young men to serve as spiritual leaders in their home countries. He returned to Korçë in June 1933, aged 27, and at once began to teach and preach, but he felt more drawn to the old "American School" set-up and dropped out in May 1937 rather than hold any responsibility beyond preaching. In August of the following year he resumed responsibilities in the mission, and began regular preaching services and Sunday School work in a rented shop in a slum section of Korça. In March 1939 he withdrew from the work again (and finally) because of "a crusading spirit against certain secular practices" which he did not share: we say this with no blame; we do not even know what those practices were. But his time in Austria sealed his fate later on, as we shall see.

Koço Tili

Koço Tili was born in Korçë to an Orthodox family, and enjoyed going to the Orthodox services as a child until 1933 when his father became ill, and there was no-one else to take him to the services. Eventually, a friend invited him to go to the Evangelical meetings, and he began attending every Sunday morning. By now he was about 12 years old. He noticed that a lot of young people went, including ones older than himself. He enjoyed listening to the sermons, and his regular attendance enabled them to find a lodging place in his heart. He was also impressed with the seriousness and love with which Phineas and Violet Kennedy received the youngsters. When he was about 16 or 17 years old, he also began attending the preaching with the adults. As time went on, the Spirit of God worked in his heart, and he took part with other Albanians in preaching in surrounding villages—Turan, Ravonik, Dvoran, Drenovë and others, following guidance given beforehand by the missionaries. Those who took part in such evangelism were mainly Ligor Çina, Niko Tasellari, Kristaq Treska, Bajram Bektashi, and Koço himself. This way of life continued till 1940, when the missionaries left.

The late 1930s

Left: Nikolla Çeno and Edwin Jacques with literature outside a mosque

Below: Korçë youth work, July 1938

*Above: Setting off for village
evangelism.*

*Right: Nikolla Çeno during
evangelism at Shkodër*

Internment of the Evangelical Workers, September, 1938

For a period of three months the summer and autumn of 1938, not a week went by without two or three persons coming singly to the mission to confess Christ as their Saviour. Soon thirty-four of these were in classes receiving Biblical instruction in the Christian life preparatory to baptism. It seemed as though the praying and planning for the formation of an evangelical church were about to be realised.

The missionaries consulted lawyers, who assured them that there was absolutely nothing in the laws of the State to hinder changing one's religion: "The State is non-religious. Religion is purely a personal matter. Article 3 of our Constitution declares that every individual is free to follow the religion of his choice."

So the baptism of the first four was announced for Sunday, 11th September, 1938. They were Ligor Çina, Koci Lubonja, Nasi Lubonja and Gaço Xoxi, and were aged 19 to 25.

But then the government dropped its blockbuster.

Ligor Çina

The preceding Saturday afternoon, some gendarames or military police knocked on the mission gate, asking for four men by name. It looked ominous, for these were the four men scheduled for baptism the next morning. Located in their homes, they were locked up at the police station without questions or charges. Missionary intervention was useless.

The prefect assured missionary Edwin Jacques that the prosecution originated in Tirana, also that there was constitutional freedom of religion in Albania—freedom to follow the religion of their fathers, but not freedom to change their religious affiliation.

On the 13th they were escorted by guards with fixed bayonets to the bus station, put in the rear compartment of the bus with the mail sacks, and taken the nine-hour drive to Tirana, the capital. Again they were locked up.

Jacques went to Tirana and pleaded their cause before the Minister of the Interior, who had jurisdiction over religious matters, then before the Minister of Justice and the Minister of Foreign Affairs. The upshot was that "the exercise of religion in Albania is free, but proselytising propaganda is forbidden by law, and such cannot be tolerated, because it creates quarrels and disharmony among the religious elements." Also proselytising propaganda "disturbs the status quo, the religious equilibrium of the State, and having political implications it must be prohibited."

It was useless to point out that these men were not guilty of proselytising propaganda; that they had simply wanted to exercise their constitutional right to follow the religion of their choice. These four officials were Muslims.

So Jacques appealed to the Prime Minister, an Orthodox official. Following the interview, Jacques noted:

He received me very kindly, assured me that he had heard nothing of the case, and asked for details. He appeared visibly agitated, and assured me that (a) about *the arrests,* he would follow this up with the Minister of the Interior, that no one has a right to arrest the men on such charges inasmuch as the State is officially non-religious; (b) about our *rights as a mission,* we are perfectly free to receive individuals as Protestants if they are of age; (c) about the establishment of a Protestant community and Church: provisions are made in the law for the establishment of 'new' religious bodies to be recognised by the State. He advised getting in touch with a lawyer and taking steps as outlined in the law. Naturally his comments were greatly encouraging. On his discussing the matter with the Minister of the Interior however, the latter seems to have prevailed. The arrests were not reconsidered.

Apparently however 'conversions' *were* taking place in Albania with impunity. Jacques noted further:

While in Tirana I met a young man who had left the Catholic Church for Bektashism. I read of a Uniate (Catholic) priest who published in the paper a declaration of repentance so as to re-enter the Orthodox Church. And I recalled an Orthodox priest in Korcha who had turned Uniate (Catholic). It seems that this persecution of our men is outside the law, intended to intimidate our believers.

Jacques found the four men shut in a room without a ray of light. They had been moved from their earlier room, which was infested with fleas, bedbugs and body lice, and shared with an old man headed to the insane asylum. Though they had no idea what lay ahead, their spirits were good and their confidence in God unwavering.

For ten days they had only bread and water. Then, with no charges or hearing, they were told that they would be interned for two months.

The prisons were already full of Communists and other malcontents, so internees were confined to the city limits, obliged to remain in the room provided by the police from dusk to dawn, and required to report at the police station each morning. The police also made a minimal food provision daily.

The mission, with legal assistance, submitted a detailed appeal to the Minister of the Interior, but nothing ever came of it. The hostile police action seemed indeed like a blockbuster dropped on the Evangelical Mission.

Time enabled the four in Tirana and the evangelical family in Korça to see that there was a silver lining even to this dark cloud.

First, instead of picking up one of the men scheduled for baptism, Koci Lubonja, the gendarmes had got another man with the same first name who had been baptised a year earlier, Koci Treska, of whom we have written above. Friends urged the innocent victim to make known the mistake and escape the unjust punishment, but rather than involve his friend and brother in Christ, the breadwinner in a widowed family, he remained silent and took on himself the punishment due another. All recognised this as a Christlike act.

Secondly, ten other members of the baptismal training classes determined to appear in court if given the opportunity to testify in behalf of the four. That was significant, for to identify oneself with those in official disfavour could cost a person his job or his future.

Thirdly, the police advised the four one morning that to avoid monotony they should look around for a job. Asked if they could sell books, the police assured them that they could, if the books were examined first for Communism. The four immediately sent to Korça for a carton of scriptures and Scripture booklets. The police found no Communism in Abraham, Isaac and Jacob, or Peter, John and Paul. So they approved the books, although expressing doubt as to whether many people would want to buy them. For the remaining six weeks they were uninterrupted in their canvassing of stores and coffee houses for purchasers, and the distribution of free booklets. They even set up a table on the boulevard of the capital city and offered Scriptures to the strolling passers-by.

They wrote that they also asked for permission to hold meetings in their living quarters, but were forbidden.

Their exchange of correspondence with Korça friends was mutually stimulating. They happily identified with the apostle Paul, who had wanted to preach the Gospel in Rome the capital, was taken there in chains and kept in a hired house, and Caesar paid his travelling expenses!

Ligor Çina and Nasi Lubonja were later baptised in a river.

The persecution put iron in the souls of the evangelical family. Their favourite hymn in those weeks was Martin Luther's "Ein' feste Burg" ("A mighty fortress"):

> Fortes' e fort' është Zoti yn,
> Dhe e pa tundur mbrojtje.
> Mbretëron ndihmonjësi i yn,
> Nga vdekja na sjell rrojtje.
> Se gjith ay armik
> Kërkon të fut intrig;
> Të shumtë ka fuqi
> E mbushur me mëri
> Ky që mbi dhe s'ka pasur shok.

Nevertheless this unforeseen hostility was something of a blockbuster. Discussions in family circles and in coffee houses spread the impression that it was not expedient to be seen at the Evangelical Mission and to share the official disfavour. Governmental intolerance made new believers apprehensive. Inquirers had second thoughts about attending public meetings.

The survival of the Mission, the missionary outreach into the region, the baptism of new believers and the organisation of an Evangelical Church: all these seemed in jeopardy.

Those intolerant officials, so ready to crush a small evangelical minority, could have no way of knowing that a gathering whirlwind would destroy not only their religious minorities, but even their Muslim majority! For Albania would become the only thoroughly atheistic State in the world. That Muslim intolerance was but a faint shadow of the intolerance yet to come. During the years when evangelism was done, the Bektashis received workers in their teqes, conversed with them, and said the Gospel was near to their own faith. It is not that they were really interested in the Gospel itself. They were openhearted, and loved to converse about what they and the evangelists believed. The Kennedys had many friends among the Bektashi dervishes and visited them regularly. Actual response to the Gospel came from among the Orthodox. There were only two or three converted Moslems: Tefik Mborja, Bajram Bektashi and a girl who sang in the choir.

Bajram Bektashi

Bajram was scheduled for baptism with the other four mentioned above, but as a sergeant in the army he could not get leave on the proper weekend. A few days later he came to Korça, learned of the arrests, and had the courage to go to the police station and identify himself as another who had accepted the Lord Jesus as his own Saviour. Edwin Jacques told the story:

By the way, I did not get this story from Bajram himself. It came right from headquarters. One evening in the market place I heard a voice calling, 'Zoti Xhejks!' ('Mr. Jacques!'). A gendarme came up, a Muslim and a good friend. With a grin he asked, 'What are you doing to these men?'

Then he told how Bajram had visited the police station, indignant over the other arrests. He declared that he too should be arrested then, for he likewise was converted to Christ and awaiting baptism, but could not obtain leave that day.

The gendarme continued, 'Bajram is a good man, though, and my wife comes from his village, so we hushed up the matter.'

Later Edwin Jacques wrote:
As Italy and Albania were about to declare war and I left last June, Bajram was the last of our group whom I saw. Our Italian military truck stopped at a roadside camp. There was Sergeant Bajram, caught in the iron military discipline of Fascist Rome, marching with his machine gunners to the Yugoslavian frontier. As we said our *natën e mirë's*, there in the starry chillness of the mountains, it was a consolation to know that here and there in Albania's night are those redeemed ones—blameless and harmless, the sons of God without rebuke in the midst of a crooked and perverse nation, among whom they shine as lights in the world.

He was enlisted by the Italians, and died in the Battle of Crete.

After the Awakening:
the Evangelical Community in Korça

The War Years

During the Second World War, Albania was occupied first by the Italians (who invaded on Good Friday, 1939), then by the Germans.

Edwin Jacques, the last missionary to leave, in 1940, was involved in training a small group of men and women to continue the meetings. There were at the time about a hundred Evangelical believers in Albania. Many Christian men died resisting the Italian occupation, and when the occupying forces were driven out, it was hoped that a new day of freedom had dawned—but it turned out to be the beginning of a new and long bondage under one of the most oppressive Communist regimes mankind has produced.

Meetings were held in the house next door to the mission where Nikolla Çeno and his mother Stojna lived, which belonged to the mission.

The Sunday School ceased to function after Edwin Jacques's departure.

Ligor Çina and Nasi Lubonja were imprisoned for doing evangelism in the villages, which the Italians thought was anti-Fascist propaganda. They continued selling Bible books among the villages into 1942. They were in the village of Leshnje near Vithkuq when some police wondered whether they were distributing political propaganda. They were taken from Leshnje to the town hall in Vithkuq, examined and taken in a commandeered vehicle to prison in Korçë. There they remained for almost three months with no questioning, and were released when it was agreed that they had only Bible portions.

Koci Treska was interned in 1940 by the Italians as a lover of the Americans, and held for some weeks at the carabinieri headquarters. He refused to deny either his faith or his American brethren.

The Italians used the mission as a prison. Outside the mission gate to the left there is a bronze plaque stating that the Germans used the building as a prison for captured partisans, and that the partisans' colleagues in the mountains stormed the place under cover of darkness and enabled them to escape to the hills.

As the Jacques' received the story, because Nikolla Çeno knew German from the Bible School near Villach, Austria, the Partisans enlisted him to work as a double agent. Appearing to collaborate with the Germans, he learnt when they had intercepted plans of partisans to visit their families in the city, and he could get a warning to them to flee before troops surrounded the house and captured them. They owed him their lives. With his access to the German offices, he could also overhear plans for troop movements and pass on word to the guerrillas. But this had to be super secret, as both the Germans and the Albanians had to believe he was working sincerely. Later he paid dearly for his service to his countrymen.

Towards the end of the period of German occupation a bitter three-cornered civil war broke out between the Royalists, who sought the return of King Zog, the Balli Kombëtar (National Front), and the Communists, led by Enver Hoxha. The Communists claimed to be the main group fighting the Germans, and it was British policy to provide them with ample military supplies; much of the material supplied was in fact used against the other Albanian groups, and after November 1944 (when the last German forces withdrew) Albania became a Communist state led by Enver Hoxha who ruled till his death in 1985.

The post-war Period: Communism

By 1945 the Communist régime was already beginning to put restrictions on Christian and Moslem organisations. A large number of religious leaders were interned, imprisoned or executed, often being charged with collaboration with the Fascist occupiers. Other clergy were assigned to work which the new régime regarded as "productive". Many of those committed to labour camps and prisons were priests. Persecution of the Roman Catholic minority has been well documented: it was ruthless and bestial. We know less about the sufferings of other religious groups. In 1967, all remaining 2000+ religious buildings were closed, and Albania declared itself an atheist state. Enver Hoxha argued that Moslems had collaborated with the Turkish invaders; Orthodoxy was a tool of the Greek Government in its imperialist intentions; and Roman Catholic clergy had welcomed the Italian invaders. He therefore claimed to be abolishing religion for patriotic reasons, and in order to unite the people.

There was evangelism in the villages during the War and until 1947, and as far as villages round Gjirokastër, in the period 1945-7, done by Kristaq, Ligor and Nasi. Small groups came, literature was sold and explained, and there was preaching and personal work. Then such work was forbidden.

The school and mission were taken by the Communists and used as a dispensary for the health service. Later, it was used as a dwelling for the poor. No rent was taken, because it was known to be the property of the American missionaries. Part of the building was demolished.

After 1947, people burnt their New Testaments for fear of the Communists.

Meetings of the Evangelical community were held in private houses. As the situation worsened, they had to be held secretly, but

they never stopped. They met usually twice a week. From 1947, four
to ten people were in attendance. The meetings included preaching,
singing, prayer. Much help was derived from the hymns. The Lord's
Supper was not celebrated after Edwin Jacques's departure. Believers'
children did not attend, for fear they should be a security risk.

The leaders were Ligor Çina, Kristaq Treska, Koci Treska,
Nasi Lubonja and Koli Qeramexhi.

Nikolla Çeno was killed by the Communists. When the Germans
withdrew, local people were unaware of his true work as a double
agent protecting the partisans, because it had had to be so secret. So
in 1945 he was taken by the Communists and shot on 15th June as a
German spy. He was posthumously exonerated by the Albanian
Parliament in 1993 and declared a Martyr for Democracy. An article
was published about him in the newspaper *Korça Demokratike* in July
1993. It reported that

> Judge Nevzat Haznejdari, without so much as a quiver in his voice, condemned
> Çeno to death for collaboration with the Germans ... The only misfortune of
> this intellectual was that he knew German and was known as the only person in
> Korçë at that time ... For almost fifty years, his family lived under the drama of
> scorn without seeking even the most elementary human rights, because they
> were cruelly punished by the Communist society. His daughter was deprived of
> the right to live with her husband, an endless suffering which can drive you to
> insanity... He himself remains buried in an unknown location, for the only
> fault that he knew German.

Ligor Çina reported in a letter written in 1993 that Nikolla Çeno's
wife and daughter moved to Tirana and lived with her parents.
Stojna Çeno, Nikolla's mother, died in great poverty, but remained a
believer till the end.

The church continued to meet with Koci Treska as preacher, twice
a week, Wednesdays and Sundays. We give some details of believers'
experiences under Communism, supplied by Koço Tili:

Irakli Katro kept his Christian faith. During the Italian occupation
he opened a workshop for the production of rubber shoes. All his
property was confiscated in 1946, he was imprisoned as a rich man
and intellectual. He died in 1948.

Elemi Lako, being wealthy, had all his property confiscated and was
forced to work as a simple workman, painting from town to town to
earn bread. He kept his faith and died in 1980.

Ollga Plumbi was born in 1898 in a village near Përmet. In 1930 she came and taught at the American mission school, and joined the Partisans in the mountains in 1943 during the Italian occupation. After the War she was chosen to head the Albanian Women's Organisation, but she was against Communism and did not accept its totalitarian principles. A year later she was replaced by Enver Hoxha's wife, but she was never imprisoned, and died in 1948.

Praksithe Plumbi was a Sunday School teacher with the Evangelical Mission and was the Jacques' language teacher. She was dismissed from her post as a teacher in 1946 on the pretext that she was pro-American. She remained with no pension. The Communists persecuted her with psychological pressure and spied upon her continually. She died in 1948, a good Christian.

Ilke Shosho was born in 1917. He came twice a week to the mission prior to the clamp-down and was well loved by Phineas Kennedy. Also, during the years 1934 to 1940 he often met with Edwin Jacques, and sobbed when Jacques left Albania. He remained an Evangelical believer. He died of cancer in 1943. His brother Gaqo disappeared in 1943 at the hands of the Communists.

Viktor Gjogoreci, being pro-American, was killed by the Communists in 1944.

Lefter Kosova was an officer during the Italian occupation and was spied upon by the Communists. He was a minister for a short while, and the Communists killed him at the door of his home as an anti-Communist and alleged spy of the SIM, the Italian secret military police.

Pandi Plasari was tortured by the Communists in the early years of their régime.

Eli Emanuel studied at middle school in Romania 1932-1936. During the Communist time his whole family were persecuted, his father and a brother were imprisoned and all their wealth confiscated. He remained unemployed and unmarried. In 1993 he was still alive and following the Lord.

Konstandina Poda went to Tirana in 1945 with her family. She was a good Christian, but her husband became a Communist and was in the military choir. One of their daughters was a Christian. Konstandina died in 1962.

Sotiraq Qirjako: all his parents' wealth was confiscated by the Communists, he was imprisoned for six years; he lived as a simple workman in Kavaja.

Pandi Sovjani remained a believer. He was left in unemployment and found work where he could. He was still alive in 1993, but died later in a road accident.

Hari Panariti remained a good Christian. During the Italian occupation he was head of the Chamber of Commerce helping the poor. In 1945 he was arrested as pro-Italian and as an intellectual and was condemned to twenty years imprisonment and interned in Burrel. He was released from prison blinded and died shortly after. He remained a good Christian till death.

Taqi Skendi became a Communist right at the start and a close comrade of the Dictator. He became Minister of Health. He was still alive in 1993, but paralysed.

At least two or three turned away from the faith. Another, whom for his family's sake we shall not name, became a Communist at the very beginning and spied upon his fellow believers. He died despised by the population in 1968.

Koço Tili was mobilised as a soldier in Gjirokastër in 1945 or 1946. Various Communists spied upon him, and he was imprisoned as an Evangelical with the accusation at his trial that he had been a spy for Phineas Kennedy. He was condemned to three years in prison, and put in a cell in Gjirokastër castle but was released after a few months. He remained unemployed, but was permitted to study Economics. After completion of these studies, he was not left in Korçë but transferred to Sukth, Lushnjë, Kuçovë, Maliq and Bilisht, and in each place he was watched him and followed with a view to imprisoning him again. In Lushnjë he was accused of having been an Orthodox priest. Throughout all these transfers, he managed to retain his copies of the scriptures and other religious literature, but when he visited Korçë the other believers no longer knew whether he could be trusted. He seldom met with them during that time, but their sign was to wink with one eye to say, "I am still a believer in Jesus." Koço only went two, three or four times secretly to Koci's house during the Communist years, and met four or five times with Ligor Çina. They spoke of their faith and of the missionaries they had known. He met Kristaq Treska more often, as they lived near each other. It was necessary even for those who hated the Communist régime to praise it in public.

Koço died in his native Korçë on 28th January 2006.

Koci Treska

In 1948 the Communists arrested Koci for gospel work in Korçë, and for listening to foreign broadcasts (BBC, Voice of America). He was kept by the secret police for 4-6 months in Korçë and tortured, as evidenced by the blood on his clothes which his mother took home for washing. He kept silence about his colleagues, despite an offer of liberty if he informed. He was sentenced to seven years imprisonment, and served three of the seven years. He was made to break stones on a road gang.

All his life after the war, till about 1973, he worked at physical labour. He also gave private lessons in English and French, but charged little money, taking whatever people gave him. But people were afraid to associate with him, because of the attitude of the authorities, who viewed him as an enemy. This, coupled with the discrimination against him after the war on the part of the authorities, the smallness of his pay and later of his pension, reduced him and his family to the extreme poverty in which he eventually died. He wrote to David Young on 1st April 1991 saying:

Very beloved brother David,

My stomach is very bad, I have pain day and night. I cannot sleep. We are in a very bad economic situation. I can say that I am dying of hunger. I hope you can send me some food ... sugar, honey, milk, butter, biscuits, cocoa, chocolate, sweets ... I did not receive the thick winter coat ... I believe you will do all you can to fulfil these requests. Forgive me for troubling you beyond measure.

Nine days later, on 10th April, he wrote again:

Yesterday I received the parcel of food. Do not worry. Nothing was lost. I harassed you. I ask you to forgive me... As for my health, I have pain day and night, I can neither sleep nor eat. May God put His hand upon me!

A few weeks later, on 16th May, he died, passing into the presence of the Lord whom he had loved and served for so long and at such personal cost. He was widely known as "Koci Shenjtë"—St Koci.

Contact re-established

Until Albania opened once more to gospel work in June 1991, nobody knew what had become of the small Evangelical community.

From the middle of 1990 the Albanian Evangelical Trust (later renamed Mission), via its links with Dr and Mrs Edwin Jacques, was able to be discreetly in touch by post with the remaining group of believers in Korçë. David Young gave our first missionary, Mike Brown, their names and addresses, and Mike visited them whilst in Albania with a tourist group in April 1991. He wrote:

"I was the first expatriate to minister to them for 50 years. They showed me where the mission used to be.

The main building has now been demolished, however three of the buildings (now houses) still remain, including the house the Kennedys used. They also showed me the schoolhouse in which Sevasti Qiriazi [1871–1949] used to teach 'way back in the 1890s.

"Each of them has a very strong, clear faith in the Lord. Each had kept copies of the scriptures secretly and read them. They each have a strong desire to "get things going again" and start

1991: David Young (right) with Skender Dako, Sevasti Qiriazi's son.

preaching the gospel, and were distributing the scriptures I gave them.

"Ligor [Çina] continually stressed the greatest need is for "a pastor, a teacher, somebody from outside" to come and live there and start the work over again. When asked what we could do to help, he simply said to send somebody here to preach and teach and to send scriptures in.

"So, there is a handful of believers there who are desirous to start rebuilding again. We need to go and start! I would suggest very forcibly that the work in Korçë take first priority above everything else."

In God's providence the Communist régime ended about two months later, and by early July Mike Brown had responded to the need for a pastor and teacher expressed so strongly to him just a few weeks earlier, and himself became pastor of the Korçë church. Some account of the new period of blessing at Korçë and of new churches being established in many other towns is given in the book *Mission to Albania*, compiled by the Albanian Evangelical Mission and published by Christian Focus.

In 1993 Ligor Çina wrote:

I remember we used to go with Nasi, sometimes also Mr Konrad, to the villages around Korçë. It was a joyful work—for Christ says that the sower went forth to sow—in such a way that that seed, which was planted then, has results now in the present time. I sometimes go to the villages and I remember my youth, which was so joyful.

Left to right: Ligor Çina, Koci Treska, Kristaq Treska in 1991.

Tomorrow you die

1973

In 1973, a young New Zealand woman called Reona Peterson, and her friend Evey,[1] were clearly directed by the Lord whom they loved and served to join a tour group to Albania, then boasting of having achieved the status of the world's first atheist state. Three years later, in 1976, the story of their visit was published under the title *Tomorrow you die* (Bible Voice, Inc., USA). Loren Cunningham, International Director of YWAM, wrote in the Foreword that "To exalt Reona and Evey to be extraordinary would be to miss reality. This is the story of two ordinary girls on a dangerous mission in obedience and faith in an extraordinary God."

God used the book widely and lastingly in creating a sustained movement of prayer for Albania, which in Britain began in 1976, the same year as its publication, and which continues to this day.

Here, reprinted by permission of the author (who retains the copyright), are some extracts, unaltered, from Chapters 10 to 13 of the book, with the prayer that God will use it again to ignite a love for the Albanian people and a determination to count the cost, and then be willing to pay that cost in bringing them the Gospel of our Lord Jesus Christ.

---

1 Evelyn Muggleton

Appointed To Death

Evey woke just before seven. Propping her head in her hands, she looked over at me and said, 'Are you feeling all right? You look awful!' I told her I felt awful and that it had been a long night. Being a well-trained professional, she had slept soundly and was totally unaware of my discomfort. However, there was nothing she could have done, and she needed to sleep in order to be strong for the solo assignment that was about to be hers.

I was still unsure of exactly what God was asking of me.

So we prayed together and, like Gideon, I put out a fleece. If in the next thirty minutes I had no recurrence of pain or discomfort, I would take it as the green light to attempt the two-day tour. If, on the other hand, my condition was unchanged, I would understand I needed to remain at the hotel.

During the next thirty minutes, there were frequent spasms of pain. Therefore, I accepted my condition and asked Evey to explain the situation at breakfast. This she did. When she returned to gather her belongings for the two-day expedition, we realised what a closely knit team we had become and how difficult it was for us to contemplate separation even for two days. Several of the group came to say how sorry they were that I had to remain behind. Mary gave me some tablets that she was sure would help, and the guide relayed a message that he had left instructions with the hotel staff to take good care of me.

The group departed early, and I began to make up for some sleep I had missed the night before. I was dozing lightly when, at about eleven o'clock, a knock at the door caused me to respond, more asleep than awake, with 'Come in.' I heard the rattle of cutlery, and a member of the hotel staff entered and placed a tray of food by my bed. (I had asked Evey to be very firm when explaining the fact that I was not interested in food and unable to eat it. But I had already learned that the Albanians equate hospitality with food. Several times members of the group had not felt hungry and had declined a particular course on the menu. The waitress would then bring another type of food, thinking they disliked the first that was offered to them. It was very difficult to convey the fact that it was lack of hunger, not lack of enjoyment of the food, that was the problem.)

The smell of salami and highly spiced soup did nothing for my queasy stomach, but I turned to smile at the woman who brought the tray. As I did this, I realised I was looking into the face of the woman God had shown me in the vision while I was praying in a small group in 1970! My heart began to pound, and I prayed to God to give me time so that I would know what to do.

About one o'clock there was another knock at the door.

I said 'Come in.' The same woman entered bearing yet another tray of food. She put it beside the untouched first tray and then she did an unusual thing. She sat down on my bed, took both my hands in hers, and just looked into my eyes. I knew what I must say. Slowly and with fervency I said, 'Marx, Lenin—No! Jesus—Yes!' Tears came to her eyes, and leaning over she embraced me and said in very limited English, 'Me Christian too!' I gave her a copy of the Gospel of John. She began to read a verse out loud, then she laughed and cried at the same time. After a few minutes, she reluctantly slipped it into the pocket of her black uniform, picked up the first tray and left the room to continue her cleaning duties in the hotel.

I fully expected her to return; so when at four in the afternoon there was a loud knock at the door, I called out, 'Come in!' In came a man of about fifty. In broken French he said he was from ALBTURIST and I must come with him. At first I thought I was not hearing properly, so I asked him to repeat the sentence. I had heard correctly the first time. I explained that I was ill and could not come with him. He replied that he would wait outside while I put on a coat; but I must go with him. He scarcely gave me time to find my clogs and slip on a dressing gown before he opened the door and beckoned me to follow him.

Down the long corridors of the hotel we went until we came to Room 201. I am sure there had been a rise in my temperature and a quickening in my pulse as I walked down the corridor seeking to take in what was happening. But many times during the early days of the tour, I had remembered the words God had quickened and the understanding that he had given—that the road ahead was not an easy one—and I had wondered just how it was going to come to pass.

He pushed open the door of a small room, into which were crowded five men. Three sat behind a table. The windows were closed, and the air was already blue with smoke. They pointed to a chair directly in front of the table, and I sat down. It became obvious very quickly that the men in the room performed different functions. One was an interpreter, one was to act as a scribe to record all the proceedings, one was the official from ALBTURIST, and three had come through that afternoon from Tirana to conduct his interrogation. These three were members of the Ministry of the Interior.

They began by asking straightforward questions: name, nationality, occupation. They presumed that because I was with a French group, French was my mother tongue. I hastened to explain that this was not so and that I needed an English interpreter. This displeased them and forced a temporary halt in the proceedings. The French interpreter left, and in his place came the English-speaking guide from the Norwegian group. She was a temporary replacement until an official interpreter could come through from Tirana.

Her eyes grew wide when she saw I was the accused and she said coldly, 'I don't believe you could do such a foolish thing!'

We began again. After the preliminary questions, a copy of the Gospel of John was placed on the table and the chief interrogator, a man in his early forties, asked me if I had ever seen it before. I replied that I had seen one like it, if not it. He then said, 'Your friends have exposed you.' I asked him which friends he meant and he said, 'Your friends in the tour group.' I told him that was impossible. I had only one friend in the group, and she would never expose me because she loved me.

Into my mind flashed the incident that had occurred in an Eastern European country during the past decade. Several pastors in a town were arrested simultaneously and brought in separately for interrogation. Each one was told that another pastor in his town had exposed him. One after the other, their reply was identical: 'That could not be so. That pastor is my brother. He loves me. He would never expose me.' When all had been interrogated, the man responsible for their arrest said, 'How is it possible to have such love and loyalty? I want what these men have.' The memory of this story brought strength and comfort to my heart.

With a cynical sneer, the chief interrogator said, 'Don't talk to us about love; what is it anyway?'

It must be remembered that the entire interrogation had to be interpreted—the interrogator's questions from Albanian into English and my answers from English into Albanian.

Without further reference to my friends in the group, one of the men said, 'The person you gave this booklet to exposed you.'

To this I had no immediate answer; but in the following days, I was to receive understanding. There is little doubt that the Gospel that lay on the table was the one I had only a few hours earlier given to the hotel worker. Was she a Judas? Had she really betrayed me? I was never able to believe this. Her subsequent behaviour reinforced my conviction that she was a true believer, my sister in Christ.

Several times in the next two days she came to my room weeping quietly, and just hugged me, taking my hands in hers and squeezing them tightly. Because the room was now bugged, she knew better than to say anything. I had also to remember that it was God who first showed me her face and gave me to understand that I would meet her. What actually did happen only eternity will reveal. In her joy and excitement did she show it to another hotel worker? Did it fall out of her pocket? Did she leave it lying about somewhere? Was it discovered in her uniform pocket when she changed her clothes?

With considerable restraint and gentleness, the chief then urged me to answer their questions simply and honestly. 'If you tell us the truth, no harm will come to you.'

I told him that would not be a problem as I was accustomed to telling the truth. The questions now concerned where I had obtained the literature and how it had been brought into the country. I realised they were clever men, phrasing their questions in order to trap me. I began to think carefully about my replies. This angered them, and to my surprise, one of them began to glare at me and shout, 'Liar! Traitor!'

It was then that God flooded my mind with the words from Luke 21: *Don't be concerned about how to answer ... I will give you the right words and such logic that none of your opponents will be able to reply!* (TLB) From this moment, I ceased to labour with my own mind and began to prove the truth of the promise. What peace of heart and mind resulted!

Without warning, their gentle approach ceased, and they began to demonstrate great anger. The chief thumped the table and roared like a lion while his friend, the one who had shouted, 'Liar! Traitor!' left his chair and came over to me until his nose was almost touching mine. He proceeded to babble in Albanian, combining much spitting with his talking. Normally, such treatment would have made me afraid; but the louder and angrier they became, the more peace flooded my being. I could not understand it. At the same time, instead of feeling repulsion for these angry men, I felt genuine, deep love in my heart for them. The louder they shouted, the softer and more gentle my replies became. It really was possible to love your enemies and bless them that curse you; to pray for them who despitefully use you and persecute you!

When their display of anger did not produce the desired results, they tried a third technique. The chief began by pointing to me and talking at length to the others in the room, obviously about me. At intervals, they would throw their heads back and laugh heartily. None of this conversation was interpreted. It must have continued for some fifteen minutes. During this time my spirit was not disturbed. There was so much 'liquid love' in my heart for them, I consciously had to restrain myself from smiling back at them. I understood for the first time why there are so many injunctions in Scripture not to fear—to be not afraid—for true to the promise, God was holding my right hand; he was helping me; his perfect love was casting out all fear.

The Communist interrogators aim to do one thing: to make you afraid. When they produce fear in the heart of a victim, they have secured a major victory; for fear paralyses and destroys. Nothing worries them more than to find their various techniques not producing the desired result. It was possible to read this in their faces; it angered them, frustrated them and wearied them. In an outburst of anger the chief had exclaimed, 'You will be here a long time. You are not co-operating! We will keep you here *until you break!*', ... until you break!' These were his exact words. Then I remembered the Word of the Lord that Ken Wright had brought: *'You will not break; you will not crumble.'*

It was now early evening, and by this time they were leaving the room one at a time, presumably to eat and gain new strength for the

attack. Physically I was weak; I had not eaten in twenty-four hours.
But what was this inner strength I was so conscious of? My mind
was alert, my heart was at peace. How gloriously true—'When I am
weak, then I am strong!' At this point, the English-speaking
interpreter from Tirana arrived, and the tour guide was relieved to
be able to return to her group. She gave me a long, searching look as
she left the room. Her replacement was a young man in his late
twenties. The questioning continued. What had made me come to
Albania and do such a thing? Did I not know that no one in Albania
believed in God? Did I not know that the Bible was a forbidden
book in the land? Who had sent me on this mission?

There was a knock at the door. In came a photographer complete
with an impressive array of ancient equipment. The flash attachment
was huge. Following orders from the chief, he began to take a series
of photographs. Attired in my dressing gown and clogs, I was
required to sit, to stand, to walk. I was then photographed with the
interrogators, then with the interpreter. This surely was going to be
front-page news in the Tirana Daily! This took some time, and then
the questioning resumed.

Another knock at the door interrupted proceedings. Two poorly
dressed men entered. They appeared to be nervous and afraid. After
some introductory conversation, the chief pointed at me and asked
them a question. They both nodded their heads affirmatively. The
chief then asked me if I had seen the men before. When I told him I
had not, he seemed to ignore my answer and went on to say: 'These
are the men who witnessed your crime; as a result of their testimony,
you are condemned.'

It was difficult to believe these things were really happening. To me
it seemed more like a pantomime than an official interrogation. Just
as these two witnesses had appeared to be totally mystified by what
was happening and very afraid, the scribe was also having difficulties.
He seemed to be the most uneducated man in the room. Instead of
an impressive pad on which to record the proceedings, he had an
odd collection of pieces of paper; and his one pen refused several
times to write. At one point, he leaned over towards me and with
sign language asked if I had a pen that he could borrow. On another
occasion, they stopped and asked him to read back what had just

been said. He was so far behind, it was impossible for him to oblige. He then became the target of their anger.

It was now past midnight, and the interrogators were showing signs of fatigue. Of the three men, one had been strangely reserved and quiet throughout the proceedings. His opinion was obviously valued, as he was always brought into the discussions. Unlike the other two, he had a kind, gentle expression and a real softness about his manner. Many times, following a question, he would lower his gaze so as not to look directly at me. I felt convinced that my Christian testimony was not falling on deaf ears. When the beads of perspiration stood out on my forehead, the gentle interrogator suggested they bring water and let me wash my face. Water was also brought for me to drink.

They had a consultation together; and then with considerable dramatic effect the chief began to ask me, 'Do you have a father?'

'No,' I replied. 'He is dead.' 'Do you have a mother?' 'Yes.'

'Do you have a brother?' 'Yes.'

'Do you have a sister?' 'Yes.'

'Do you love them?'

'I love them very much.'

There was a considerable pause...

Then the chief said, 'You will never see them again. You are a traitor to the glorious People's Republic of Albania, and traitors are shot. We will come for you at nine tomorrow morning.'

I heard what they said, but again there was no disturbance within my spirit.

Then the chief looked at me curiously and asked, 'Did you understand what I said?'

I could only reply, 'Yes, I understood what you said. You said that you would come at nine tomorrow morning and shoot me!'

There was a long silence. God chose this moment to imprint a verse of Scripture on my mind and heart. Throughout the following hours and days, it would flash its truth to me like a highly charged neon sign. If I myself had chosen a verse to sustain me through this time, I don't believe it would have been this one; but God chose it for me—and in his infinite wisdom, he knew what I needed most. It was the first phrase of Psalm 31:15: *My times are in thy hands* (KJV).

It was 1.00 a.m. We had been in this stuffy little place for nine hours. They led me back to my room. They went to my suitcase and turned it upside down. Then they stripped the beds, poked large needles into the mattress, pulled everything out of the closet, and took my handbag and emptied out the contents of the two side pockets. They took possession of whatever portions of Scripture they found, including my English New Testament and my *Daily Light*. Surprisingly, one of the interrogators produced a sheet of tissue paper and carefully wrapped all the Scriptures in it.

Feeling that it had been a job well done, they moved to the door. The chief was the last to leave. He simply said, 'We know that you are an agent from the Vatican. If only you would confess to this, we would not have to shoot you.' I'm sure my mouth dropped open with amazement. At the time, I did not understand how they could imagine such a thing. Only later did I learn that the Christians who resisted, even unto death, the measures to remove every vestige of religion from the land were members of the Roman Catholic Church. Just months before we entered the country, in a labour camp, a priest had been found secretly administering the sacrament of baptism to a baby brought to him by its mother. He was shot at a public execution. The news reached the ears of the Pope; and one of Italy's major newspapers printed the story with the request from the Pope to Catholics worldwide to pray for the Church in Albania, which he called 'the Church of silence'.

Anyone who would do such a fanatical thing as I had done must surely be a Catholic. This must have been the reasoning of the interrogators. I reminded them that they had urged me to speak the truth and that I was truthfully telling them I had no connections whatsoever with the Vatican or with the Catholic Church. 'Then we will see you at nine tomorrow,' were the chief's last words. He closed the door behind him.

I now knew what a ransacked room looked like. I dropped to my knees beside my dishevelled bed and began to pray, 'Lord, I believe I need to sleep. You promise in your Word that you give your beloved sleep, and I believe that in this situation I am beloved by you. Thank you for the gift of sleep.' I then moved all my belonging off the bed to the floor, found a sheet, pulled it over me and lay down. Sleep came immediately.

Fear none of those Things
which thou shalt suffer

Tuesday, 2nd July. The hotel was strangely quiet, but then I was its only occupant. It was seven o'clock. I had slept for almost six hours. The first thought in my mind upon waking was, *They will not come for you at nine. They will come much later in the day. This is part of their psychological warfare. You have much time to prepare.* Only God could bring such understanding.

I first restored order to the room; then still feeling physically weak, I lay down on the bed and began to say aloud certain Scriptures that I could remember. I meditated on them and then made them the substance of prayer. Earlier—during the night—just after the interrogators had left my room, I heard the noise of a cord being dropped along the ceiling and considerable activity going on in the room above me. Everything pointed to the fact that a listening device had been planted. I wanted to give them something to listen to; so after meditation and prayer, I began to sing the many precious Scriptures in song that I had learned. Oh, how they ministered life to my soul, even as I sang!

If this was to be my last day on earth, how should I spend it? Would this be the day of my entry into the presence of the King of kings? Then what should I be doing to prepare to meet him? I discovered what a realist God is. He seemed to be asking me, *What is it that you will find difficult to leave behind?* I thought seriously about this, and then I realised what a blessed individual I was. I had so few possessions—none of them would be hard to part with. God had allowed me to remain single in order to serve him more effectively; there would not be the pain of parting from a husband or children.

What, then, would be difficult? Just leaving behind my family and friends. At that moment I understood why the Lord Jesus, as he hung upon the cross, looked toward his beloved mother, Mary, a widow, and said to John, 'Behold your mother.' And to Mary, 'Behold your son.' For I felt God saying to me, *Give them to me one by one, these that you love, and I will take care of them.* I began with the most difficult, my widowed mother; then with the other members of my family; then with my most precious friends. Having done this, I experienced a release of spirit and heart and mind that was totally new to me.

Such joy and praise welled up within me, and I found myself saying out loud: 'Lord Jesus, it will be a privilege to lay down my life for you. You are more precious to me than houses or brethren, or sisters or father or mother, or husband or children or lands.' In this way the morning passed into the afternoon.

I was resting quietly when, without warning, I became conscious of an evil presence in the room. Into my mind flashed a direct and urgent question: *How important are you to God that he should rescue you out of this situation? What have you ever done for him and for his kingdom to warrant being released?*—There was only one possible answer: *I have not done anything to deserve his favour!*

Then came a second question: *Those friends who promised to pray for you—are they keeping their promise? You've agreed many times to pray for people and you have not always done it. And if they are praying, are they like you so often are—too lazy to be led by the Holy Spirit in prayer? I could only reply, I don't know. I don't know whether they are praying. I don't know whether they are in touch with my situation.*

I found these questions and the answers that followed exceedingly painful. Then it was that God came to my rescue. Into my mind flashed another precious and powerful truth—one I had known for some years, but now it broke with new revelation on my soul, and I found myself speaking with confidence and conviction. *It could be that not one human being is aware of my situation and is praying* (I was later to learn that the opposite was true—prayer, informed prayer, was ascending from God's servants in many nations on several continents), but one thing I knew: the Lord Jesus Christ, who spent thirty years in obscurity, then three-and-a-half years in dramatic public ministry, has for almost the last 2,000 years—to the exclusion of all other ministries—been engaged continuously in intercession. 'For Christ is not entered into the holy places made with hands, which are the figures of the true; but into heaven itself, now to appear in the presence of God for us' (Heb. 9:24, KJV). And he knows exactly what is happening. He cares and is able to deliver me.

Then a cold clamminess seemed to pervade the atmosphere, and I felt my throat muscles begin to tighten. I struggled to breathe. There could be no doubt as to the source of this intrusion. I began to recall the spiritual weapons God has given to his children in order to deal with situations like this one: the shield of faith, the sword of the

Spirit, the blood of the Lamb, the Word of our testimony, the name of the Lord Jesus Christ. In prayer, I used them all; but they brought only momentary relief. Then I felt God whisper, *Sing my praise— Declare my victory to the hosts of hell.*

I had never felt less able to sing. Into my mind flashed Psalm 27:1: 'The Lord is my light and my salvation; whom shall I fear? The Lord is the strength of my life; of whom shall I be afraid?' (KJV). I squeaked rather than sang. Then I remembered Micah 7:8: 'Rejoice not against me, O mine enemy: When I fall, I shall arise; when I sit in darkness, the Lord shall be a light unto me' (KJV).

By this time, my throat had loosened and I was singing.

The third Scripture I recalled was Psalm 68:1: 'Let God arise, his enemies be scattered' (KJV). I sang it through twice, rejoicing in the almightiness of my God. Whatever it was that had entered my room left it just as quickly, and I was a wiser Christian. I had learned for the first time the effectiveness of the sung praises of God. I had entered into the experience of the psalmist in Psalm 149:6: 'Let the high praises of God be in their mouth, and a two-edged sword in their hand.' It was not that the other weapons were less effective; but rather, that God was desiring to add another one to my armoury. Many times since that day, I have proved its mighty power. It is possible to sing our way to victory!

At four o'clock there was a knock on my door. I opened it. The interpreter greeted me politely and asked me to follow him. In the few short hours the day before, in which he had translated for me, I had come to appreciate him deeply and had prayed for wisdom and for an opportunity to share more adequately with him. Room 201 welcomed us again. It was the same group of men, with the exception of the official from ALBTURIST. He was not present at all the second day.

They inquired about my health and whether I had slept well. The chief then took up the attack again. With a smile, he said, 'We knew all along that you were not from the Vatican. We know who you are. You are an intelligence agent, sent to spy on our land and our people.' This was so ridiculous that I smiled as I declared that this was not true. The chief grew serious. He leaned across the table and, pointing his finger at me, he hissed, 'I am a professional and you are a professional too!'

I remembered an incident that had occurred in the life of Corrie ten Boom, the wonderful Dutch saint, who was imprisoned by the Nazis for aiding Jews. She too was facing an interrogator. 'Miss ten Boom,' he said, 'You must tell me everything. I may be able to do something but only if you do not hide anything from me.' It was then that Corrie realised that all his friendliness and his kindly concern were devices to elicit information. The man was a professional with a job to do. Corrie commented, 'But I too, in a small way, was a professional.'

During this second period of questioning, we covered almost the same ground as the day before. No doubt they were interested in whether I could give the same answers twice. The literature was again produced; and this time they read through *The Way of Salvation* booklet and commented among themselves concerning it. The chief then said to me, 'Surely you don't believe the Bible. Why, it states that if someone smites you on the right cheek, you are to turn the other one to him also.'

I smiled and said I did believe the Bible was the inspired Word of God and that when you understand and believe that love is the greatest power at work in the universe, that verse presents no problem. To this, the chief sneeringly replied—almost in the words of King Agrippa—'Are you trying to convert us?' I realised that I was not dealing with men who were ignorant of God nor the teachings and claims of his Son, the Lord Jesus Christ.

Interestingly, they never once threatened to destroy the Scripture booklets; rather, they took exceptional care, even to the extent of wrapping them in tissue paper. The burden to pray for the distribution of these booklets throughout the land is still on our hearts and on the hearts of those who pray for this nation. We firmly believe they are still in circulation.

Our tour group was scheduled to return in the early evening. I had left a note for Evey under her pillow, and I prayed that she might find it. I felt sure that she would be brought in for questioning also.

As the evening wore on, the men became impatient. The chief complained, 'You refuse to co-operate with us. You refuse to tell the truth. We will imprison you for life.' A chill went down my spine. Life imprisonment in the nation of Albania! More grace was going to be needed to accept this than to accept the death sentence.

For the last time they asked me the question, 'Who sent you to Albania?' Again I replied that I was a Christian who loved and served God, that I had come at his command, and that I was prepared to bear full responsibility for my actions. I had known, when I crossed the border, the possible implications of what I was doing.

One of the interrogators then asked an interesting question: 'Are there other people like you who are doing what you are doing?' Without realising the impact of my reply, I said that yes, there were hundreds who were responding to the call of Jesus Christ to go to the uttermost parts of the earth—to the areas that have never heard—to difficult and dangerous lands, behind the so-called Iron and Bamboo Curtains; in short, to reach the entire world with the gospel of Jesus Christ.

Undisguised fear was written on his face as he asked a further question, 'You mean others like you will come to Albania?' I told him that the command of the Lord Jesus was 'into all the world'—and that included Albania.

Angrily, they led me out of Room 201. It was eleven o'clock. The interrogators lingered inside. While I waited in the corridor, the door of Room 202 opened. It was identical to Room 201. Behind a table sat several men. To the right sat Evelyn. She looked out as I looked in and our eyes met in a long and meaningful embrace. We smiled. Many times in the course of the evening, she asked both the Albanian guide and the interrogators, 'Where is Miss Peterson?' Their consistent reply was, 'She is all right'; but they would give no more information than that.

As a result of this moment, I believe I know what it must have been like to be in the crowd when the Jewish leaders gnashed their teeth in rage because of the simple presentation of truth by Stephen. 'And he, full of the Holy Ghost, looked steadily into heaven and saw the glory of God.' The imprint of divine glory must surely have been mirrored in Stephen's face.

When I looked at my friend Evey, there was a radiance about her that spoke of the beauty of the Lord Jesus. In the midst of heat and smoke, of blasphemy and anger, she sat serenely at peace with God and man. These men may well forget the faltering words we were able to speak, but will they ever be able to forget the visible demonstration of the reality of the life of the Lord Jesus? I believe Saul was never able to erase from his memory the moment when the life of Stephen was given so recklessly and therefore so powerfully to God. Did the beauty of that uplifted face haunt him until he too met Stephen's Lord on the Damascus road? To reach a nation for God, one must aim at its leaders, its government, its men of influence. How gracious of God to give us close to twenty hours with six of the key men in Enver Hoxha's party!

My room looked the same as when I had left it, except for the addition of Evey's overnight bag. However, during this period when we were both being interrogated, the films were removed from our cameras and, most probably, a further search of our luggage was made. (In both of our suitcases was a film already exposed, and this was overlooked by them. We therefore left with films intact and were able to develop them, once back in Switzerland.) I lifted Evey's pillow. There was the note undiscovered. I tore it into tiny pieces and dropped it into the waste-basket.

There was a gentle tap on the door. Outside stood the French guide. In a nervous whisper he asked, 'What is wrong? What are they doing to you?' I pointed to my lips and then to the ceiling, and we scurried into the unoccupied room next door. He told me that when neither of us were at supper he had become alarmed. One member of the group had seen Evey walking along the corridor with the Albanian guide, who appeared to be agitated and upset. The French guide told me that he had gone to the staff of the hotel and demanded to know what was happening; but nobody would tell him anything. He had decided to stay up all night if necessary and to maintain a watch outside our room in the hope that we would be returned. When he heard the footsteps of the interrogators bringing me back, he had hidden in the bathroom. Now he waited to hear all that I could tell him.

As simply as I could, I explained our reason for coming to Albania, that we were guilty of the act they had accused us of and that we were prepared to accept the responsibility for our actions. I assured him that none of the other members of the group were implicated in any way. He did not rebuke or scold me. Instead, he identified closely as he shared the real reasons why he had come to Albania. Then he paused and said, 'But to do a thing like this, your faith and belief in God must be very deep?' It certainly was an unorthodox witnessing situation; but I welcomed the opportunity to share by both my life and my words the reality of the Lordship of Jesus Christ.

I told him that Evey was being interrogated in Room 202 and that her belongings were still in our room. We agreed together that it was most unlikely she would be returned to be with me again. Realising this might be my only opportunity, I asked our guide to notify our friends in Switzerland of what had happened immediately upon his return to Paris; and he assured me he would do this. Then in typical French fashion, he kissed me on both cheeks and said, 'Vous êtes brave, vous êtes courageuse; je vais faire tout ce que je peux pour vous tirer d'affaire. ' ('You are brave, you are courageous; I will do everything I can to rescue you.') With this we parted; he to maintain his vigil and I to sleep. I lay for some time thinking about the events of the day.

Were these clever men bluffing? Would they dare to carry through either of their threats—death or life imprisonment? Could it be that through laying down my life a man like Saul of Tarsus would come to know and serve Christ? Then my death would surely not be in vain. I could not expect the world to understand this; in human terms it would appear such a waste of life and ability. But then I recalled the saying that, in the 1950s, had challenged a young American called Jim Elliot to go as a missionary and subsequently to lay down his life for the Auca Indians of Ecuador: 'He is no fool, who gives what he cannot keep to gain what he cannot lose.'

Did I really believe that for the Christian the grave has no sting and death no victory?

And what if it were to be life imprisonment? What were the jails of Albania like? Would there be anyone there who could speak English, or would I be forced to live in a world without communication? Would they allow me to work in the fields or the factories, or would I be classified as dangerous and confined to a solitary cell? Would they give me back my New Testament? How would they attempt to indoctrinate me? Would their methods be physical, as well as mental and emotional? Did I really believe that I could do all things through Christ who strengthens me—even to living out the remainder of my life in a prison in this hostile land?

What attempts would my family, friends and country make to procure my release? Would they be able to bring sufficient pressure against such a militant government?

To what extent did this Communist nation value the increase of tourism and tourist money? Would this be a factor that would cause them to modify their punishment? Did they fear the effects of our particular tour group returning to the West with alarming tales of the arrest and retention of two members of the group?

If these men really believed that God did not exist, then why were they so afraid of the Word of God? Why did they classify it as 'propaganda'? Why did they not immediately destroy the literature they recovered from our room? Why bring tissue paper to wrap it in? What did they intend to do with it?

In the midst of such thoughts, I fell asleep.

Father, Glorify Thy Name

I woke with a start. Had I been dreaming? No, the room really was filled with people. I looked at my watch. It was 4.30 a.m. There was Evey, with three or four men—presumably her interrogators—and her interpreter. She looked tired and a little pale, but she managed to smile at me. They commanded her to open her luggage and, as with me the night before, they went through all her belongings carefully. They demanded that she give up any remaining Scripture booklets. Faithfully, she endeavoured to comply with their demand. When they later searched her handbag and found in a back pocket one more *The Way of Salvation*, they exploded with anger. It was useless for Evey to try to explain that this had not been deliberate but was a genuine oversight.

Their performance was almost identical to the night before. However, they had forgotten one thing: the previous night I was alone in the hotel, and their ranting and raving were for my benefit only. But now the tour group had returned, and many of the rooms on the floor were occupied. As I lay in bed, listening to the men question Evey, I became conscious of light footsteps in the corridor outside. I knew one set belonged to the French guide. But who else had been awakened and was listening to the performance with him?

This time, addressing us both, the interrogators announced, 'You have one more opportunity to tell the truth before we are forced to imprison you. That will be in the morning!' They opened the door and were surprised to find a cluster of people outside. The French guide with real boldness demanded to know what was going on. We heard him say, 'I have a right to know. I am responsible for them. I am their leader.' He was firmly told that explanations would be given in the morning.

Mary was also in the group. Rather than talk in our room, I went back with her and simply explained what had happened. She was afraid of being personally implicated because she had often been seen with us, and I had to comfort and assure her that this was not so. She had nothing to fear. Her room-mate listened as I spoke. I knew that she was a committed young Communist, and I wondered what effect my words would have on her. Mary was visibly troubled as she said, 'I am a Christian, but I knew better than to bring my Bible.' She was convinced she would not be able to sleep a wink. Again, I attempted to reassure her that all was well.

Looking back now upon this incident, I believe it was a major reason for our release. The fact that several members of the group had witnessed this scene in the early hours of the morning meant that if we were detained, the story of what could happen to a tourist would begin to circulate. As in most Communist countries, tourist money is eagerly sought; adverse publicity could markedly reduce this.

I returned from comforting Mary to find Evey stretched out on her bed. We hugged each other; then I knelt beside her, eager to hear all she had to share. She began first with details of her two-day journey into southern Albania.

With as much literature as possible stuffed into her brown leather handbag and into the large front pockets of her dress, Evey had boarded the bus for the journey into the heartland of Albania. The scenery rivalled anything that had been viewed previously. Quite without warning, a deep narrow valley would give way to an expansive horizon of plains. Here, where only a few years ago small flocks of sheep and goats foraged among thorn bushes and stunted shrubs, vineyards and fruit plantations now blossomed. Then from the plains, the ascent began into high forested mountains …

———⇒ ⇐———

The group returned to Durrës in the early evening, a little ahead of schedule. Evey raced up the stairs, eager to find out how I was. Her first impression, as she entered the room, was how tidy everything was. I must surely be recovered; perhaps I was down at the beach or having supper in the dining room. She set out to find me. Walking towards her along the corridor was the Albanian guide. He looked distressed as he said, "You must come with me."

A beautiful thing had occurred during the two-day trip. As our group numbered twenty, we were paired off on the bus. Evey and I normally sat together. Now she was alone. So, too, was the Albanian guide. Thus, Evey invited him to sit with her. There was so much to talk about and so much to learn from him concerning the land and the people. Unlike so many other members of the group, who were frustrated and angry about the many cancellations and changed schedules, Evey was happy to be in the land and genuinely interested in learning all she could about the country—grateful for his assistance and concern for the welfare of the whole group. The Albanian guide was obviously impressed. Before the trip was completed, he changed from using the French 'you', meaning a person in general, to a much more intimate 'you', meaning a member of the family or close friend. Certain members of the group picked this up and questioned Evey about it. She could only reply that he must be regarding her as a friend. It was therefore painful for him to be sent to arrest her.

As they walked along the corridor he exclaimed, 'But I cannot understand it! You are an educated person! You are a scientist! How can you believe in God?'

Evey replied, 'That is not difficult for me. Every time I help to bring a new life into this world (Evey is a midwife), I am a witness to a miracle of God. I cannot but believe in him.'

Firmly entrenched in the minds of the interrogators was the belief that I had forced Evey—indeed, paid her!—to accompany me on this mission. She was only an accomplice. Because of this, through the eight long hours of questioning, Evey was presented with a significant opportunity to give her own personal testimony of the detailed leading and guidance of God. She affirmed her willingness to bear responsibility for her actions. Her simple, direct answers unnerved them. When they resorted to blasphemy and vulgarity, Evey spoke to her interpreter and told him that she found their blasphemy offensive and would he ask the interrogators to cease using this sort of language. Nervously, the interpreter conveyed her request. They responded in anger. Evey believed they continued to use the same language but the interpreter did not translate it.

This incident occurred after I had been returned to my room and Evey was using my interpreter—the young man whom I had grown to appreciate so much.

At one point, they produced an impressive collection of papers. Then they said to Evey, 'You are not nearly as clever as Miss Peterson. She has told us everything; this is all the evidence she has given us.' Then, producing two or three pieces of paper, they said, 'This is all you have told us.'

Evey replied, 'I'm not clever, but I am honest.' We have laughed many times at the possible interpretation of her answer: Miss Peterson is clever but Miss Muggleton is honest!!!

For almost every question that was asked, Evey managed to bring God into the answer. Exasperated at last, they thundered, 'Don't mention the name of God again!' They phrased their next question to her, 'Who sent you to Albania?'

Evey replied, 'I am sorry, gentlemen. I know you have asked me not to mention the name of God again; but if I am to answer your question truthfully, I have to say, "God sent me".'

It was already daylight, but we had so much to share with each other. We discovered we had been asked the same questions; but, alas, to many key ones, we had given different answers! We both had spoken the truth, but this would be difficult to explain to the officials. For example, they asked me what my occupation was, and I said I was a secretary. They asked Evey what I did, and she said I was a teacher. Both answers were true. They asked me where I met Evey, and I said I had met her in Ethiopia. They asked Evey where she had met me, and she responded in England en route to Afghanistan. We had met in both these places. They asked me where I had obtained the literature, and I said it had come to me from Holland and Germany. They asked Evey where it had come from, and she said from England. (Because the literature was printed in England, Evey presumed that was where I had obtained it.) We were deeply aware that we were in an impossible situation.

In all their searching they had not discovered Evey's diary. In it was a detailed account of where we had left the literature. This had to be destroyed. It would be unwise simply to tear it into small pieces and throw it in the waste basket. I had bought a box of Albanian matches for a friend who collects matchboxes. Gratefully, I began to burn the incriminating pieces of paper. Now there was a charred mass in the washbasin. I turned on the tap—alas no water! Then I remembered it was turned off last night. How unprofessional we were at such things! We trusted that we would be undisturbed until the water was turned on in the morning. The smell of smoke was strong. We opened the windows wide and sprayed perfume in the air.

We prayed before attempting to sleep. We told the Lord we recognised that without his help we were in a hopeless position. We confessed that we did not feel very brave or heroic. We asked him, through our weakness, to manifest his strength. We thanked him for the grace that he had already given, for the peace that reigned within our hearts—even as the interrogators sustained their threat to imprison us. We told him our eyes were upon him and that we trusted him for all that the third day of interrogation would bring.

The steady, regular breathing from the adjoining bed told me that Evey was already asleep. I closed my eyes and remembered, 'In time of trouble he shall hide me in his pavilion. He shall set me high upon a rock so that my head shall be lifted up above my enemies' (Ps. 27:5).

The noise of people walking in the corridor outside our room woke me. My first thoughts were of the ashes in the washbasin. I turned on the tap and removed every trace of the burned paper. Should I join the rest of the group for breakfast? No one had said I couldn't. Evey was still sleeping. I entered the dining room, and the French guide motioned me to join him. Several of the group noted my entry, but no one joined us at the table. I was still without an appetite, but I enjoyed the good strong coffee. Giving an outward appearance of being ultra-casual, I brought him up-to-date. Between mouthfuls of scrambled eggs, he told me of his intentions to bring every possible pressure to bear to secure our release. I told him how grateful I was for his attitude and concern.

The group was to leave at nine for a day's excursion down the south-western coast to visit the much talked-about Mao Tse-Tung textile factory at Berat and the Roman ruins at Appollonia close by the city of Fier.

When I returned to the room, Evey was awake. We agreed that whatever the day held, it would not be dull—that was certain! We recalled a New Year's Eve message given by Don Stephens, the European director of Youth With A Mission. He had spoken from 2 Kings, chapter 2, concerning the hard thing that Elisha asked of Elijah. He challenged us to ask God a hard thing for the New Year of '73—something that was far bigger than we were. Evey and I had both done this, and it had set the tone for our year. Now we were in a very hard place facing a very hard situation!

There was faith in our hearts to ask God for deliverance. We could recall many Bible verses in which God had promised this thing. Verses like Psalm 91:15: 'Call upon me in the day of trouble: I will deliver you and you shall glorify me.' Why was God not giving us the liberty to pray this way? We waited in silence before him, and he spoke the same thing into both our hearts: *It is your right, as my children, to ask for deliverance. My Son was in a similar situation. His soul was troubled and he said, 'What shall I say? Father, save me from this hour: but for this cause came I unto this hour. Father, glorify thy Name'* (John 12:27,28, KJV).

God was asking us whether we trusted him enough to leave the situation in his hands. Were we really concerned with his glory? Could we truly say, 'Father, glorify your name. You know whether you can best do this by our death, by our imprisonment, or by our release. We leave that decision with you'? The prayer of relinquishment was what God was longing to hear from our lips. His grace was made available. We each prayed out loud, using the other as a witness, and we relinquished our lives to him.

A knock at the door occurred simultaneously with the end of the second prayer. Our French guide stood outside and said he had been sent to fetch us. A meeting was to take place with the other members of the tour group in a downstairs lounge.

No Weapon that is formed
against you shall prosper

As we walked along the corridor with our guide, other members of the group came out of their rooms and walked in the same direction. Our worst fears were realised—*the group was being punished for our crime!* It was now eleven o'clock, and they should have departed two hours ago. Our destination was a large room on the ground floor. At the head of the room was a long table, behind which sat several of our interrogators, our Albanian guide, the minister from ALBTURIST, and a new face—the chief prosecutor of the land.

The group assembled, a curious mixture of expressions on their faces. Some looked fearful and apprehensive, others mystified, not a few impatient; and one relaxed member (apparently oblivious of the night's proceedings) laughed as he said in a loud voice, 'What's this? An interrogation or something?' The chairs were spread in a semicircle facing the table, and Evey and I sat with the French guide a little to the left of centre.

Conversation ceased and the prosecutor rose to speak. The Albanian guide interpreted. At length, and with considerable dramatic effect, the official began his speech. He expressed his sorrow to the group for their detention and then went on to explain that, unknown to the Albanian government, two members of this particular group were criminals who had crept across the border undetected. Once in the country they had committed crimes against the glorious People's Republic of Albania. The eyes of the group turned toward us. Many expressed shock and amazement.

After a moment, the prosecutor spoke again, 'Will the two criminals please stand.'

We stood. This must surely be an effort at public humiliation. Then came the declaration of our crime. We had smuggled religious propaganda into the land—portions of the Bible in the Albanian language—and distributed it throughout the country. There was an almost audible expression of relief from the more tense group members, ardent socialists though most of them were.

The prosecutor continued, 'We have seriously considered how to punish these criminals. They are guilty and therefore worthy of imprisonment. However, because they are young girls (this was quite flattering), we have decided to release them. We will drive them to the border and leave them there, declaring them to be *personae non grata*' (i.e., not able to enter Albania again).

Evey had been faithfully interpreting the prosecutor's speech into English for me. But my ears were not prepared to hear this! Had she interpreted it correctly? Were we to be released. Could it be possible?

I was still trying to take this in when one of the group got to his feet and said in quite angry fashion, 'I demand to know what is wrong with bringing Christian literature into the country!' This was unbelievable! I was thinking how marvellous that such a challenge should be given; but Evey was concerned lest they think that others were involved in our crime.

A real hubbub broke out, with considerable interchange in Albanian and French. I believe that for many it was an opportunity to vent some suppressed frustration and anger. Members of the group began to come over to us, especially the women, and express their love and concern. Some inquired whether we had sufficient money to get home. Others wrote out their names and addresses in France and handed them to us. One woman even remarked, 'You have done this because your faith in God is real.'

Without warning I felt the tears begin to flow. At no other time had I come remotely close to weeping; and to be honest, now I was a little embarrassed by it. Our chief interrogator saw it and seized the opportunity to say, 'If you had thought more carefully about your actions, you would not have to be crying now.'

How could he be expected to understand that these were tears of joy and gratitude to God for his love and grace—not the tears of self-pity and remorse that he suspected.

A further announcement was made. The group would depart immediately on their tour, and we two would go to our room and pack our suitcases. The police vehicle was waiting outside the hotel to take us to the border. The authorities had intended this episode to dishonour our credibility and defame the name of Christ. Instead, God had presented us with an unparalleled opportunity to share with our entire group our reasons for being in the land. When death to self has taken place, public humiliation is not difficult to bear. Identification with the Saviour, who in his humiliation was denied even justice, was a very real privilege.

We bounded up the steps, two at a time. When safely in our room, we hugged each other and danced and sang. Within minutes we had packed our belongings; but what would we do with our Albanian leks? The only things for sale at the hotel were postcards; so while I set off to purchase some, Evey wrote a short note to our friend Helene. She was Mary's room-mate, the brilliant young student from Paris. She was with us the night we went into Durrës; and because she was fluent in English, we had enjoyed her company on the bus, at meal times, and on other occasions. We had learned that she was a student of economics and languages and, although only seventeen, she had already completed her first year of university study. When questioned about her philosophy of life, she had shared that she was committed to Marxist-Leninist principles and that she had been able to spend time as an exchange student in Russia. She spoke Russian fluently, as well as French and English. We had noticed that she had limited pocket money. Therefore, Evey put some leks in an envelope with a short note, urging her to buy a souvenir with it. Evey also gave her our home address. It was a simple matter to slip the envelope under the door of her room.

As I walked toward the lobby where the postcards were displayed, I was surprised to find the chief interrogator and the interpreter walking toward me. With an undisguised sneer, the chief said, 'So you thought you were free! There are more questions we require you to answer. It depends on how you answer these further questions whether we will release you or not.' They commanded me to return with them to Room 201. The moments that followed were exceedingly difficult. The announcement of our release had resulted in a total relaxation… of mind, heart, body and spirit. I was to be freed!

Must I now enter into combat again? Had the announcement so dramatically given to our tour group been just a fabrication of lies? Had they been fooled into believing we would be released? Now they had departed. The authorities were free to do with us as they liked, and no one would be the wiser. The thought was chilling!

The chief's opening remarks were, 'Your mission is an absolute failure. But you are a professional, and we cannot afford to let professionals go so easily. We will wait for Miss Muggleton to join us. Then we will proceed with further questioning.'

Within a few minutes Evey arrived. We looked at each other without smiling. They spoke first to Evey. 'Are you responsible for your actions?'

'Yes,' replied Evey, 'I have told you many times that I accept this responsibility.'

The interrogators continued. 'But Miss Peterson shall keep responsibility.'

Evey looked at me and was sharply commanded to look only at the interrogators. We were told we were to have no communication whatsoever between ourselves. She replied, 'No, we each accept responsibility for our actions.'

They said firmly, 'No, Miss Peterson shall keep responsibility.'

Did the interpreter find it difficult to translate clearly into English, or were they saying what we thought they were saying? One of us was more guilty than the other. It was not possible to share responsibility. They would consider acquitting one, provided the other could be declared guilty. They then began to repeat questions they had asked us so many times before—to which, if pressed to an ultimate point, we would have to reply, 'I am not able to give you that answer.' Questions like: Who had sent the literature to us? How did we happen to both be in countries so far apart as Ethiopia and Afghanistan? What school did I teach at?

It was at this time that we witnessed a marvellous thing take place. As they phrased their questions, we knew what they were leading up to. Yet, as they would approach a critical point (after laying a careful foundation), they would immediately—without any explanation—veer away and begin to ask a completely new set of questions. This happened not once, but every time they came close to a question to which we were not willing to give them an answer. We recalled Loren Cunningham's prayer: 'May there be a release of God in the land.'

I believe these intelligent, highly skilled men must even today recall with pain, embarrassment and wonder their endeavours to solicit the truth. So many times they reminded us of deflated balloons as, filled with self-importance and arrogant confidence, they hurled their questions at us, only to crumple and deflate as the wisdom of God left them without reply.

The scribe then produced a huge bundle of papers. This was all the written evidence that had accumulated during the interrogation. Each page had to be translated for us and we were then instructed to sign it. Evey and I had identical pages. This took a considerable amount of time and put a real strain on the interpreter.

Then, in contrast to the mass of papers that were written by hand, an official-looking typed sheet was produced. The chief addressed me and said that this was a list of the crimes I had committed against the People's Republic of Albania. Evey did not have one of these sheets. I was asked for my signature, so I requested that it be translated. Strangely, they refused this. I replied that I could only sign it when it had been translated. Again they refused. Were we about to have an ugly confrontation? I felt Evey stiffen at my side. I sent up an arrow prayer, 'God, if I sign this, I could be signing my death warrant.' The answer from heaven was swift and direct: *Sign it and trust me.* Another arrow prayer, 'But, Father…' And another swift reply: *Remember, your times are in my hands. You are not at the mercy of these interrogators.* So I signed the statement.

The interrogators left the room, and the scribe asked, rather apologetically, if he could go over some of the evidence to make sure his English was correct. Did we imagine it or did he purposefully single out the paragraphs that contained our Christian testimony as the ones he needed to have us explain more fully? For several minutes we answered his questions. How we did appreciate the help he had given us, and we were grateful for the opportunity to express this to him!

A hotel worker appeared and the interpreter explained that a meal had been served for us in the dining room. This really surprised us. It was now two o'clock on Wednesday afternoon. My last meal had been Sunday supper. I could not explain my lack of hunger nor my adequate physical strength; but with the announcement of the meal, my appetite returned. We sat alone in the very large dining room, being served a three-course dinner.

We were still uncertain of what they really intended to do with us. It was possible that they planned to separate us, perhaps to release

Evey and detain me. But we were learning to recognise and appreciate God's intervention in the present and to trust him with the future. Our meal completed, we returned to our room, collected our belongings, and then made our way to the police car parked at the entrance of the hotel. It was not quite what we had expected. A driver was labouring with a crank handle to start an ancient Volvo.

We still had a considerable amount of Albanian money which would be worthless to us should we be released from the country. When our interpreter appeared we told him this and asked if we could change it. Our minds said, 'Of course not; it's useless even to ask such a thing!' When the vehicle finally coughed and spluttered into action, however, we drove first to the Adriatica Hotel; and in a matter of minutes our Albanian leks were returned to us in the form of French francs. This was the first real indication that maybe they did intend to release us. But would we both taste freedom—or would the joyous release of one be tempered by the retention of the other?

The police car was very obviously a four-passenger vehicle. Yet six crowded into it. The chief interrogator, Evey, myself, and the scribe sat in the back seat—in that order. The driver and interpreter took the front seats. Why did we have such an important escort? We knew that for the first few kilometres the road that led to the northern border also led to the capital, Tirana. For which were we bound? That was the all-important question! Our first stop after the Adriatica was a petrol pump, and then we began the journey.

Prayer was more important to us than conversation. While our escorts talked among themselves, we again took our place of authority over all the devices and strategies of the Evil One. There was no doubt in our minds that a battle was being waged at this very moment in the heavenlies. What joy to know that 'far greater is Jesus Christ in us than all the combined power of the principalities of darkness.' We renewed again our relinquishment of the right to be delivered—if God could be more greatly glorified by our imprisonment or death.

I had often wondered what it would be like to be in a difficult or dangerous situation and unable to pray aloud. Was silent prayer just as effective? Now I had the answer to my question. Our four Albanian friends were oblivious to the fact that prayer was being made to

God—that defeats were being handed out to the hosts of wickedness in heavenly places. Evey and I were not only conscious of spiritual victories taking place but, as we prayed, encouragement, strength and peace flooded our own souls.

We had driven for about thirty minutes, when the chief interrogator thumped the driver on the back and the car screeched to a halt. A large truck had appeared in front of us, and workmen, with an assortment of shovels, spades and pickaxes in their hands, were jumping off. Their work for the day must have ended; but why were they being left here? Would they walk the rest of the way to their houses? This appeared to be a road junction of some importance.

Then, both back doors of our car opened and the chief and the scribe got out. They gave us a brief nod and then slammed the doors shut. The driver started the engine, and we took a sharp turn to the left, entering an empty road. No explanation was given to us, and we did not dare to ask for one.

Could it mean that we were now on the road that would take us to the border? Had we left the scribe and the interrogator on the road that went to Tirana? Would they hitch a lift to the city? Was it possible that we were both going to be released? Once earlier in the day, we had relaxed prematurely. We would not make the same mistake twice. Was this indeed the road to Shkodra that we had travelled by night on our first evening in Albania? Everything was unfamiliar; we had no way of knowing where we were or where we were going. Could there be a prison for criminals who smuggled propaganda into the land somewhere in the northern regions of the nation?

After about an hour, the interpreter spoke sharply to the driver and we stopped suddenly. On the other side of the road, several vehicles were parked—mainly trucks. Behind a high hedge was a tea garden of sorts. Roughly hewn tables were attached to wobbly legs. Long planks served for benches. So many feet had trampled the ground that the grass long ago had been reduced to bare earth. The interpreter ordered four cups of tea, and we drank gratefully. The place was hot and dusty, and the police car emitted powerful fumes which had served to dry our mouths and throats. As we sipped our tea, we became objects of curiosity—two foreigners travelling in a police car with a two-man escort! That was not a normal everyday occurrence!

We drove on. Two men jumped onto the road and commanded us to stop. The pig disease again! We left the vehicle while it laboured through the strip of straw. Then it was our turn to walk through it. In my enthusiasm, I stomped too heavily and plunged up to my ankles in foul-smelling disinfectant. My distress was immediately recognised. A roadside worker came with a bucket of water and poured it over my foot and then over my clog, and he and I laughed together about it. In spite of his efforts, however, my clog now bore a permanent memory of Albania etched on its suede!

We resumed our journey, approaching a populated area.

Was this the city of Shkodra? It looked as if it could be. Yes, it was—there was the austere and crumbling Fortress of Rozefat dominating the city. So we were travelling directly north. The border of Hani Hotit could only be, at the most, an hour's drive away. Then an unhappy thought came to me: Would the same guards be on duty at the border as the day we had entered? If so, could we expect an ugly scene with the men who had searched our luggage? We had lived through so much in the past three days—and God had been so faithful and his strength so sufficient—that if this was necessary before those massive, barbed-wire gates swung open and we were escorted into no-man's-land, we would survive!

The scenery was now familiar—the squalid little villages surrounded by fields of corn and wheat; the rustic stone bridges that allowed the mountain streams to flow on undisturbed to the sea.

The presence of groups of soldiers became more and more noticeable. The interpreter spoke with the driver. We stopped at the entrance to a military camp. Was this the one we had passed on our way into the land? Were we less than a mile from the border? The interpreter left the car and walked up the long driveway to the barracks, having first shown his pass. The driver turned on a radio and treated us to the Albanian equivalent of 'Top of the Pops'—or maybe we were close enough to Yugoslavia to be picking up one of their stations.

We waited for twenty minutes. The interpreter returned without comment, and we drove on.

Within minutes, the familiar border buildings were in view. We had never expected to see them again. The area appeared to be absolutely deserted. There were no vehicles coming or going; no men to be seen. On the side of a nearby mountain, spelled out in huge stones that had been painted white, was the slogan that had greeted us upon our arrival: PARTI ENVER. It had been almost meaningless to us when we first read it; but in the course of seven days, we had come to understand something of the power and influence upon the nation of this man who has ruled with an iron fist for over thirty years. During the tour, Mary had explained that this sign was placed at the border for the special purpose of aggravating the Yugoslavians.

It was six in the evening. Politely, the interpreter asked for our passports. We handed them to him.

We had no desire to enter the buildings or to make contact with the border officials. Alas, the drama of the day and the long journey made it necessary for us to find a bathroom. Trying to look as inconspicuous as possible, we entered through a side door. We endeavoured to explain our need to a cleaning lady, and she understood and pointed out the place. Sadly, no cleaning had been done there in a long time! We returned to the car. How long a short period of time can appear!

How large would the *personae non grata* be in our passports? Would it take up the whole page? The entry stamp had been most unimpressive—just a small triangle with the date, the name of the border, and up one side of the triangle the word Shqipëria, which means literally 'land of the eagles'. (This is the name the Albanians use to refer to their country. Of the many national dances performed throughout the land the most famous is the eagle dance done by the men.) The interpreter left the customs building and came towards the car, our two passports in his hand. Gravely, he handed them back to us. This was not the moment to look inside. He opened the trunk and lifted our two cases out. He handed them to us; and with no emotion in his voice, he said, 'You may go.' We picked up our cases and walked through the gates into no-mans-land. We did not pause to look back. We heard the gates close behind us. Was our mission a failure?

No! He, the King of Glory, would cause these ancient gates to open again! Perhaps not to us, but to others like us who would hear and respond gladly to his commission to go into all the world, particularly to the lands where Christ is not named. As it is written, 'To whom he was not spoken of, they shall see: and they that have not heard shall understand' (Rom. 15:21, KJV).

Statue of Enver Hoxha, Gjirokastër (now removed)

Zagoria

(Shaun Thompson, from correspondence with David Young, 2006–7)

We had heard some rumours about there having been a few "Evangelicals" in the mountain villages of Gjirokastër prior to Communism, but nothing very detailed, and there seemed to be some confusion as to whether they were Evangelicals or in fact Jehovah's Witnesses.

Earlier this year, I met an elderly man in Gjirokastër who claimed his father was an Evangelical Christian. He himself—the son—used to be a leading Communist official in the town, though he seems to have had a change of heart concerning his religious convictions (or lack of them) since the fall of Communism. He expressed a desire to meet again and talk at greater length. Several months passed by without us meeting—he went to Athens for an operation on his eyes, then I was in the UK for the birth of our daughter—but I finally sat down and spoke to him at some length last summer.

This former Communist expressed considerable regret at having embraced atheism, and spoke with great enthusiasm about his father, Stathi, and his faith in Christ. He seemed convinced that his father had been an Evangelical believer, having adopted these convictions during the time he worked in the United States before the War. What's more, he told me that there had been a small group of such believers in the Zagoria area of Gjirokastër district. This was exciting to hear, since previously we had no knowledge of there having been any Evangelicals in this part of Albania. These men have all since passed away, most of them many years ago, but apparently the memory of them has not. According to my elderly friend, the most prominent among them was a man named Nasho Idrizi, whom he called the *spiritual leader* of the group.

The area named Zagoria lies behind the mountain of Lunxheria, opposite the town of Gjirokastër. There are ten villages in the Zagoria valley, all of which are Albanian-speaking, and Orthodox by tradition. Most of the inhabitants have moved away during the last forty years—to Tirana, Gjirokastër, and more recently Athens—though there are perhaps about 250 families still living there.

I have made two trips to Zagoria during the last few weeks to try and find descendants of what I'll call "the Zagoria group" of Evangelicals—and to clarify what it was they believed and practised.

The road to Zagoria goes past the small town of Libohova, is all unsurfaced from that point on, and is generally unsuitable for a normal car. The 26-year-old Mercedes that I drive picked up a flat tyre on the first trip through the mountains, and I damaged the oil pump on the second, but as I said to Petrit Korbeci who accompanied me on the second trip, The soul of someone from Zagoria is worth it.

On my first trip, I met a number of elderly people who were able to give first hand testimony concerning the Evangelicals in Zagoria, including the grandson of one of the group, who sadly has become a Jehovah's Witness (thinking he is following in his grandfather's footsteps—though he still calls his grandfather an *Evangelical*). He knew his grandfather quite well, and even remembers some of the songs they used to sing. I wrote two of them down.

The most exciting moment—and I felt the most significant—was during my second trip, when I met the one surviving son of Nasho Idrizi. His name is Lusho, and though he is old and frail, his memory serves him well. He assured me in no uncertain terms that his father was Evangelical, not Jehovah's Witness. I asked him several questions to clarify this and the answers he gave were pretty convincing. I'd say he is a reliable first-hand witness. He was 25 years old when his father died and took part himself in the meetings of the Zagoria group, which his father held in the family home.

According to Lusho, there was a core group of about half a dozen believers with various other sympathisers of their faith. I'm not very clear how often they held meetings, or for how many years it continued, though Lusho did give some description of the meetings held in his father's home (he lives in the same house today). Apparently his father read the Scriptures in Greek (he was self taught) and translated them on the spot into Albanian. It seems his father would give some exposition and others would add comments afterwards. They repeated the Lord's Prayer together, but I'm not sure if there was extempore prayer also. The focus of their faith was on Christ, not on "Jehovah", Mary, or other of the saints.

They were certainly non-conformists. Although they were from an Orthodox background, and lived in an exclusively Orthodox area, it is noteworthy that they would not attend the Orthodox Church. They did not baptise their infant children. They frowned on the popular adoration of icons. They must have created quite a stir. But these men seem to have been of uniformly good reputation, which gave them credibility.

Nearly all members of the group emigrated at some stage to the United States for periods of at least several years. What I'm not quite sure of, is whether they all became Evangelicals through their contact with churches in the New World, or whether some of them adopted Evangelical convictions before emigrating. In the case of Nasho Idrizi, who by several accounts was the unofficial leader of the group, he seems to have become an Evangelical while in the United States. He was an early member of Vatra, a society of Albanian patriots in the USA, and very patriotic. He mixed with leading Albanian intellectuals in the USA, like Fan Noli and Faik Konica. However, his active involvement in the patriotic movement diminished with the growth of his new religious beliefs. I think he returned to Albania in the 1920s.

After the War, Nasho was imprisoned in Gjirokastër castle for spying. The charge, of course, was nonsense, but back in 1946, when the Communists had not yet been in power long, they couldn't imprison people for their religious convictions, because the laws against religion had not yet been put in place. Nasho actually had a debate with a Communist official who was quartered in his house, where Nasho's Christian views clashed with the Marxism of his official guest. The Communist got so upset he pulled his gun out! Lusho Idrizi (Nasho's son), who was present when this took place, said his father kept calm throughout. Nasho was arrested a few days later. In those days, if you wanted to have a mattress in prison, you took your own. I've heard the account from two different sources that on the day Nasho was released he wryly said, "I don't know why I was put in prison, I don't know why I'm being let out again, so I think it just as well to leave that mattress where it is." In other words, he knew he might be going to prison again. Nasho kept his faith to the end.

In the village of Konskë, I met the son-in-law of Peço Thimio, also a member of the Zagoria group. His wife passed away only a couple of years ago, but apparently she followed the gospel her father had taught her all through the Communist years. Interestingly, Peço Thimio taught his daughters to read and write. This was in the pre-war years of general illiteracy, when it was common even for most men in the villages to be unable to read.

The grandson of Peço Thimio also told me that his mother began studying the *Watchtower* when the family came into contact with Jehovah's Witnesses during the 1990s, and initially she thought it was the same as the faith passed on to her from her father, but after a while she said that she didn't know who this "Jehova" was whom they kept going on about, unless they meant Jesus Christ, whom her father had taught her was our Lord and Saviour. I found this an encouraging sign that his mother was in the true way of faith. She may have known little, but it took her in the right path.

One question that needs to be answered is this: Why have we heard rumours that these men were Jehovah's Witnesses? The main reason, I believe, is because of the confusion caused by Jehovah's Witness missionaries working in the Zagoria area since the 1990s. I feel that in some cases they have deliberately misrepresented themselves as *evangjelist* or *ungjillor* [Evangelical] in order to win favour with people, especially descendants of the Zagoria group, some of whom have embraced Jehovah's Witness ideas. But it is possible that one member of the Zagoria group had contact with Jehovah's Witnesses prior to the Communist era, picking up and preaching some Jehovah's Witness ideas—and this would certainly have caused confusion too. More research may clarify this.

Certainly the Zagoria group as a whole seem to have been pacifists—a well known characteristic of the Jehovah's Witness sect—but this was nothing unusual for American churches in the 1930s, where pacifism was very widespread.

Uncovering the roots of this previous generation of Evangelicals helps to show that we have history in the Gjirokastër area and are not a newly imported religion, and to know God has been at work among them in the past encourages Albanian believers. The research gives us a good reason to visit villages and helps build bridges for personal evangelism, as does meeting their descendants.

At the beginning of November 2006 I made a trip to Tirana, the capital, and met with the son of Stathi Muço (another Stathi from Zagoria). Stathi led a secret Bible study in Tirana during the 1960s. I am still trying to sort out whether Jehovah's Witness literature may have had some influence on these people, since modern Albanian Jehovah's Witnesses are calling them their predecessors. I think they make this claim unjustifiably, since this group also called themselves Evangelicals, and they had no contact with the outside world during Communism. Even if they were not very clear doctrinally, it is at least encouraging to learn of men and women who were *seeking* God's light through the Scriptures when the world around them was going mad.

Later I made a third trip to Zagoria. The main reason for going was to meet with Lusho Idrizi, the son of Nasho Idrizi, and I wanted to follow up a couple of other contacts as well.

Lusho, now 77, is a little frail after having had an operation, so I thought it prudent to make a special effort to meet him again and get as clear an account as possible of what he recalls of the Zagoria

Shaun Thompson (right) visiting mountain villages with an Albanian believer in 2006.

group. I was glad to find him standing in the yard of his house helping a younger man cut his firewood for him. After pleasantries were exchanged, I asked Lusho a number of questions about his father, some of which I had asked him previously. I was hoping that my visit of three months ago would have stirred his memory and he might have recalled some new information since then.

Lusho maintains with certainty that his father was an Evangelical and not a Jehovah's Witness. He doesn't seem to have any axe to grind of his own, so I think his testimony carries considerable weight. He was, as I have mentioned previously, present at the meetings that his father held in the family home. As for the teaching of Nasho Idrizi, Lusho recalls that Christ was the main object of his father's preaching, and a call to live a righteous life. There was no mention of 'Jehova'. His father did speak quite often of the final resurrection (something Lusho says he found hard to swallow), but he is quite sure that his father never spoke of a date for that and associated events to take place, restricting himself to the message that "it is near". Lusho tells me that his father travelled to the towns of Korça and Vlora to preach there also. This was no small undertaking in days of very primitive transport. It seems that these initiatives to preach in other towns were entirely his own. In order to do so, he obtained permission from King Zog's officials to hold an open-air meeting. Lusho says that he had a good friendship with an officer of Zog's gendarmes, who actually provided him with a gendarme as an escort to keep him safe during his travels.

Confirmation of much of this information has come from Petrit Idrizi, son of Nasho's oldest son, who is actually just four years younger than Lusho. Petrit used to be the head of education for Saranda district, and is a very fit and sharp 73-year-old. I met him in Saranda in the autumn. He used to be a Communist, but was very open to talk with me, and has asked me to visit again.

Digging round the old roots is producing opportunities for the gospel in places where otherwise there might not be any. I have been able to share the gospel with all the people I have mentioned above, and with various others I have come across while doing research.

Pastor Femi Cakolli
Messiah Evangelical Church,
Prishtina, Kosova

Pastor Cakolli's course has not (as I write) been finished, but he has set many an example of a very good beginning. What made Femi Cakolli change his faith from Islam to Christianity? How did he go from the possibility of becoming a Muslim priest to becoming an atheist? What made him change his mind again to embrace Christ? Why was he called a spy by both the Serbian and Albanian news services? Why did his neighbours call him "crazy"? Why did a Serbian journalist write a book about the group of which Femi was a part? Femi gave the following testimony to the JAVA newspaper.

Why I changed my faith—I was a Muslim then I became a Christian

A pastor's story—in his own words

My childhood and youth:
from Islam to atheism.

I grew up in the village of Krilevë in the mountains of eastern Kosova, a community of two hundred houses. Just like every child, a lot of my beliefs came from my family. Among them was my faith, the forming of my religion. Coming from a Muslim family, I inherited Islamic practices and knowledge. Even today I remember the lessons of that time: "the Muslim faith is the purest faith; the Muslim faith is the most correct; Mohammed is the last prophet and the most loved of God; every child is born a Muslim; Muslims have "Bajram", the mosque, the Koran, the priest, etc. They must pray and that's it."

Then, as I grew up in the midst of our one-time "revolutionary" youth, it was considered embarrassing to believe and practise these things, to believe in the existence of God. It was considered bad to go to the mosque or to church, because "the faith of the Albanian is Albanianism". We as a family, especially my older brothers, were illegal nationalist activists organised in different groups and influenced by patriotic and Marxist-Leninist literature, and all this served to encourage in me the idea that there was no God.

Therefore as a young man I began to regard the question of faith differently. I believed that there was no God and that nature itself is God; that the Koran wasn't a holy book; that Islam was an Arabic nationalist movement which we didn't need since our faith was Albanianism and the "word of honour" or besa was the priest of Albanianism; that the "hoxhas" (Muslim priests) are the biggest spies of Serbia; that the hoxha only goes up the minaret if paid; that science is the answer for everything.

Femi Cakolli

An attempt to become a hoxha!

My father was village hoxha, or muezzin, in Krilevë for forty years. A muezzin is a priest who calls the faithful to prayer. Through him I learned the more hidden aspects of faith of the Muslim clerics, of Islamic literature and the scale of ignorance and primitiveness of the crowds at the mosque and in life.

My father wanted me to register at the Islamic school in Prishtina. That was in 1985. I was in the second year of middle school, and I

Krilevë mosque

didn't want to go to the Islamic school. In the end, despite many efforts to get me in, I was not accepted. I remember when the commission responsible for accepting new students asked me these three questions:

    1. Do you know any prayers in Arabic? I didn't give a good answer to this.

    2. Do you have a, copy of the Koran at home? I replied, "No!"

    3. Do you want to become a village priest? I said, no. This question struck me with an unbearable irony and affront.

Why didn't I become a village priest?

Firstly, I was afraid when thinking about the future, as I was so young. When someone died, I was afraid of death and especially of old age. I knew that I would have to wash the bodies if I became a priest. Think about it, a young 18-year-old priest, washing the naked corpse of 90-year-old man. How could I manage this religious life? and what kind of God would require such a thing of me?

The second thing was that if I became a Muslim priest, I would no longer be able to hang out with my friends. I wouldn't be able to play football, swim in the river, watch sports on TV, wear the clothes I liked.

The third thing was that it seemed to me as if I was betraying the ideals of our youth who were suffering in prison for the ideals of our nation, because as a hoxha I wouldn't have as much credibility as those patriots and revolutionaries. What would I have as a hoxha? Villagers would give me formal respect; I would have with me a crowd of old people, hard of hearing, who wouldn't understand well; I would have the opportunity to receive money from anyone who died in my province, and I could expect offerings at Ramadan and holidays. In one way I understood that the call of being a hoxha would isolate me from life, from youth, from ideals, from new horizons of knowledge, from the freedom which I dreamed I had in the depth of my spirit, and if I accepted this fate, afterwards I wouldn't have anything to take pride in, either as a young man or as an Albanian.

I often thought about writing a book about these events. Up until I had finished middle school, I hadn't known that Albanians were also Christians as well as Muslims. I didn't even know anything about other nations. I thought that all people were Muslim, apart from the Serbs. Influenced by the Islamic worldview, my hate at that time towards the Serbs was simply because they were "of the Cross" and not because they were our enemies and oppressors, this I learned only from the patriots.

The first Albanian writers were priests

In 1989 I arrived in Prishtina to study Albanian Literature, mostly because I wanted to learn about the spirit, literature and history of our culture. I now found a great dedication to reading various books of my own choosing, at the same time listening to various professors, taking part in meetings and symposiums, and living in an atmosphere of youth. These influenced me in thinking I could find answers to my questions through analysis.

I also came up against some new questions in my mind. I was living in a dormitory and sharing a room with an Albanian Catholic from Stublia e Vitisë. Through my studies of our literature and history, I learned that at one time all Albanians had been Christians and that there were also still Christians today, that the Catholic church existed even in Prishtina, that our national literature for about three hundred years had been written almost exclusively by either Catholic or Orthodox priests. Zeal for my studies of ancient Albanian literature during my first year led me to the Catholic church in Prishtina as well as to the Protestant church in Prishtina, in order to search for more religious and psychological literature.

When I learned that in fact the big mosque in Prishtina had been a church ...

Discovering these two churches awoke in me an interest in the practices of Christian life. In the meantime I came across other pieces of information, such as the fact that the big mosque in Prishtina had been a church two hundred and eighty years before; that Pjetër Bogdani, who studied theology and philosphy at Rome and became bishop of Shkodër in 1656 and Archbishop of Skopje in 1667, was buried in its yard; that the National Theatre had been a church; that another church had been knocked down in Prishtina and in its place another building put up; that there were still many families secretly practising their Christian faith, even though to others they were Muslims.

Another thing I noticed was the difference between the religious rituals of the church and those of the mosque, the difference between the priest and the "hoxha", between the Bible and the Koran, between Christian culture and Islam, between the West and the East. At the Catholic mass I had seen young people, girls and children, whereas at the mosque you see mainly old men. The priest speaks Albanian, the hoxha Arabic and occasionally very poor Albanian. I started to read the book "Rrethimi i Shkodrës" by Marin Barleti. Among other things it talks about the beauty and the courage of Albanian women. As I read, I saw the Shkodran mother of five hundred years ago, beautiful, brave, patriotic, and my own mother today with her beauty covered in clothing despised by the Shkodrans, whilst the main attribute of her personality was "to be silent, to give birth, to serve."

At that time, not because I had any theological training on these things, but because of my contact with Christians and because of my knowledge of Islam, I began to see great differences. Christians, especially Evangelicals, persevere in holy living, in forgiveness, in repentance, in love, in continual spiritual freedom. This is never required of Muslims. When I started to read the Bible, among other things I encountered our own Illyrian, Dalmatian and Nicopolitan history, and it therefore seemed more familiar, whereas the Koran, which I had difficulty understanding, seemed very far away. The Bible I saw as an encyclopaedic history of knowledge of many peoples, whereas the Koran is more like an unclear Arabic biblical summary.

To become a Christian you need contact with and experience of God, whereas Islam claims to be inherited from before birth. This idea of inheriting faith is one of the biggest errors of religious doctrine, as it means that there will never be a spiritual renewal of believers. We know that things, riches, material goods, culture, etc are inherited, but not ideas or religion. In Christianity I found a greater freedom and tolerance than in Islam. There is no greater comparison to understand the difference between Christianity and Islam than with the works and life of Christ and that of Mohammed.

John and our former faith

I remembered my father and others telling me that at one time our family, which came from a village in the Leskoc region two hundred and seventy years ago, was Orthodox Christian and that John was the name of our last Christian forefather who had become Muslim. From childhood I had had a respect and great love for this name. Our forefather was John and he and I were separated by only eleven generations. In the year 1991, for the first time I had a New Testament, and one of the gospels called "The Gospel of John". This was the gospel through which God spoke to me in a profound way.

It was March of the year 1992 when I finally gave my heart to Jesus as God and my Saviour. God had given me a vision in which he called me to become his priest (separated for him, valued by him, dedicated to him). This was a personal experience and I surrendered to this spiritual call of God. I accepted Jesus into my life as Ruler and Lord. I said a prayer of salvation and repentance from sins. This was my first ever prayer to God entirely in Albanian. I experienced freedom and was touched spiritually. No one could move me in my faith in Christ. I was completely in control of this decision. Christ didn't require me to change my name or surname, neither to wear any special clothing, but simply that my life please God and that my heart be committed to him. Nor was I required to become Catholic or Orthodox, but to follow him and become his disciple.

Why did the Serbs as well as Albanians think I was working for the CIA?

I first started to proclaim my faith at the Protestant church in Prishtina and then among my family and friends. I received a harsh reaction. I had never had such a reaction before, whether speaking about Buddha or Confucius, Plato or Mohammed, Abraham or Marx or Lenin. However, when I spoke about Christ, there were strong feelings. I understood then the aspect of spiritual warfare, light against darkness. The Bible says that the darkness and the Devil oppose Christ who comes from heaven, from light, whereas the world is ready to accept whatever comes from itself. Opposition came and continues to come today, from individuals or different groups.

I remember when I was invited by some Serbian police inspectors to discuss my faith. They mocked me saying: "You were born a Muslim and that's how you should die. Why would Christ be interested in you, he belongs to us, you belong to the Turks, to the Arabs. Listen to your father. All Albanians are Muslims." The Serbian police interrogated me a few times, watched my home thinking that I was a spy for the CIA together with all Evangelicals in Prishtina. Articles against us and the Evangelical movement in Kosova were even published in the newspapers *Jedinstvo* and *Politika*. A book was written about us, in two volumes, called: *Kill Your Neighbor.*

In 1995, after hearing about this, some Albanian politicians invited me to come and talk with them. They were also convinced that we were working with the CIA. I made it clear to them that this was not the case. One of them told me: "We know who you are. You don't need to tell us." Many others, Albanians, told me that they thought we were linked to the Serbs.

The Catholics called us "Laramanis" and said that we couldn't be Christians because we weren't born Christians. Some of my friends told me I was crazy to be concerned with faith and such fruitless questions. Intellectuals called us a sect; others said I changed faith for money.

In 1996 the most important hoxha of Prishtina wanted to speak to me. He asked me to deny my faith publicly, otherwise, according to him, many other Muslims would take on this faith.

Jesus warned us that for his sake we would be persecuted and rejected. I am happy and at peace with a secure and active faith fulfilling God's two great commands: Love the Lord your God with all your being; and, Love your neighbor as yourself and spread the kingdom of God among all people. We should even thank God for opposition to our faith. What kind of faith would it be if it wasn't tested at all?

Ten years after the events described in Femi's testimony, we began to get disturbing reports concerning developments in Kosova. Our January 2006 Newsletter carried this announcement:—

Radical Islamic groups are spreading in Kosova and are building mosques everywhere. They openly make threats, have obstructed evangelism, threatened with fire-arms, attacked a missionary family in Malisheva with grenades, throw stones at churches, drive out members of their families who become Christian, and insult Christians in the street. This is only against Evangelicals, not against others. But despite all this, people are coming to Christ. Pastor Femi Cakolli writes:

We saw that last 4 months more oppositions against Christians from Islamic radical groups in whole country. One missionary in Deçan has been beaten from Muslims group. And in Malisheva whole one mission when back in USA because of Islamic attacks in them with bombs.

And in March 2006:—

"*Artur Krasniqi, Pentecostal pastor in Prishtina, writes:*
"During the crisis in 1999 Kosova was in the main news worldwide because of the war and tragedy. We asked our brothers

and sisters around the world to join us for a Day of Prayer and Fasting for Kosova on 31st January 1999. Now after 7 years many things have changed, but still there is need for lots of prayer.

"Kosova contains about two million predominantly Muslim Albanians and over one hundred thousand Serbs who are Orthodox Christians. The protestant-evangelical Christian church in Kosova is very small and under pressure.

"Many Kosovar Albanians have a hatred of Christianity as they were oppressed by the former Serbian (Orthodox Christian) régime. Albanians believe that whatever your religion is, to change it is shameful thing. Muslims who accept Christ as their Saviour will bring shame on their families and face persecution from their community.

"There are some serious attempts to isolate and consider the Evangelical Church in Kosova as a 'new sect'. The Provincial Government is proposing to enact a new law on religion that will require the Protestant church to register as religious community, with a condition on registration requiring a minimum of 2000 Protestant Christians to declare themselves as such in a forthcoming census. Many are afraid of the consequences if they publicly declare that they are Christians. It will be difficult for the church to reach the required number and comply.

"Please pray that God will intervene and that this hurdle will be overcome.

"Pressure [is] coming from Muslim Community as there have been some direct threats given in media against the churches and missionaries. Kosova is sliding to an extreme Islamic country."

Most of this book has been about people who have paid the price in the past to bring the Gospel to the Albanian people. There are others who are still paying the price, or who must count the cost and be ready to pay a high price, if called upon to do so. They face an unknown future. Stand with them in prayer; if God calls you, count the cost, avail yourself of Christ's resources, and go forth to pay whatever price is required to make Him known to the Albanian people, and to see them coming to clear faith in Him in Albania, Kosova and wherever they live.

Epilogue

Shall I, for fear of feeble man,
The Spirit's course in me restrain?
Or, undismayed in deed and word,
Be a true witness for my Lord?

Awed by a mortal's frown, shall I
Conceal the word of God most high?
How then before thee shall I dare
To stand, or how thine anger bear?

Shall I, to soothe the unholy throng,
Soften thy truths, and smooth my tongue,
To gain earth's gilded toys, or flee
The cross endured, my God, by thee?

What then is he whose scorn I dread?
Whose wrath or hate makes me afraid?
A man! an heir of death! a slave
To sin! a bubble on the wave!

Yea, let men rage, since thou wilt spread
Thy shadowing wings around my head;
Since in all pain thy tender love
Will still my sure refreshment prove.

Saviour of men, thy searching eye
Doth all mine inmost thoughts descry!
Doth aught on earth my wishes raise,
Or the world's pleasures, or its praise?

The love of Christ doth me constrain
To seek the wandering souls of men;
With cries, entreaties, tears, to save,
And snatch them from the gaping grave.

For this let men revile my name;
No cross I shun, I fear no shame:
All hail, reproach! and welcome, pain!
Only thy terrors, Lord, restrain!

My life, my blood, I here present,
If for thy truth they may be spent;
Fulfil thy sovereign counsel, Lord!
Thy will be done, thy name adored!

Give me thy strength, O God of power;
Then let winds blow, or thunders roar,
Thy faithful witness will I be;
'Tis fixed; I can do all through thee!

—John Wesley, 1703–1791

Translated from Johann Joseph Winckler, born 1670 in Lucka near Zweitz, awakened to divine truth as a student in Leipzig through August Hermann Francke, and pastor from 1699 at the cathedral in Magdeburg, where he died in 1722:

Sollt ich aus Furcht vor Menschenkindern
Des Geistes Trieb in mir verhindern
Und nicht bis in mein Grab hinein
Ein treuer Zeuge Jesu sein?

Afterword

For information about ongoing Christian work among the Albanian people please contact the Albanian Evangelical Mission, 29 Bridge Street, Penybryn, Wrexham, LL13 7HP, 01978 290138.

Web-site www.aemission.org.